The Catechism Prayer Book

Prayers Drawn from the Words of the Catechism

Rev. Mark Buetow

Editor

Katie Hill

Copyright © 2018

Higher Things, Inc.

P.O. Box 155 Holt, MO 64048

1-888-482-6630 • www.higherthings.org

ISBN: 9781982917746

Notice of copyright must appear as follows on the title page or copyright page of printed works quoting from *The Catechism Prayer Book: Prayers Drawn from the Words of the Catechism*, or in a corresponding location when *The Catechism Prayer Book: Prayers Drawn from the Words of the Catechism* is quoted in any other media, including bulletins and other parish study materials:

Publication of any work intended for commercial sale that uses *The Catechism Prayer Book: Prayers Drawn from the Words of the Catechism* is strictly prohibited without the express written permission of Higher Things, Inc.

Excluding the text of the Small Catechism itself, publication of *The Catechism Prayer Book: Prayers Drawn from the Words of the Catechism* for "congregational use," such as bulletins, bulletin inserts, bible study handouts, congregational newsletters, is granted up to and including an entire prayer. Written permission of Higher Things, Inc. should be obtained prior to digital "congregational use," such as congregation/ organization website/blog, digital prayer chain, social media.

Permission requests that exceed the above guidelines must be directed to Higher Things, Inc., Attention: Media Executive, P.O. Box 155, Holt, MO 64048 or to media@higherthings.org.

Text of the Six Chief Parts from *Luther's Small Catechism with Explanation* from *Luther's Small Catechism with Explanation* © 1986, 1991 Concordia Publishing House. Used with permission. www.cph.org.

CONTENTS

Introduction

The Catechism teaches and describes our whole lives as Christians.

In the Ten Commandments we learn of our sinfulness and our need for a Savior, as well as what good works we should do in our daily lives.

In the Apostles' Creed, we learn the holy Triune faith, hearing who God is and what He has done for us, especially since we could not do what His Law demands.

In the Lord's Prayer, we learn how to live the life of faith, calling upon the Lord for our every need using the very words and promises He gave us.

In the Sacrament of Holy Baptism, we learn that the Lord has washed away our sins, given us new birth in the Holy Spirit, and marked us as His own children.

In Confession and the Office of the Keys, we learn how to live as baptized Christians, examining ourselves and our callings in life according to the Ten Commandments to know our sinfulness, how to cry out to the Lord for mercy, and how to receive the comfort of the absolution, the forgiveness of sins.

In the Sacrament of the Altar, we learn that eating and drinking the Body and Blood of Christ means that He lives in us and we in Him and He will raise us up on the Last Day (John 6:54).

Together, the Word (the first three Parts) and the Sacraments (the second three Parts) teach us our whole life as Christians. The Catechism, covering these "Chief Parts" is thereby showing us the whole Bible. In fact, to know the Catechism is to know the whole Bible and everything you need to know to be a Christian.

How to Use This Book

This is a prayer book. Since prayer does not come naturally, it is good to have words to pray so that our wandering hearts and minds are kept to our Lord's Word and promises. The prayers in this book tune our minds to God's Word and promises, His Law and Gospel, to trust in Him for all things, using the words we learn in the Catechism.

This book is simple to use. Each day, read a portion of a Chief Part: a Commandment, Petition, Article, or question. Read the meaning a few times. Since faith comes by hearing (Romans 10:17) it is good to read these out loud and to learn them by heart. Then, pray the prayer given for that part. The prayers in this book wrap together the themes of the Chief Parts and put them into words which we can use to call upon our Lord in prayer, praise, and thanksgiving.

Most prayers will suggest a place in which you can name particular persons and circumstances. You might jot down the names and needs of those for whom you are praying in the space provided at the back of the book so that you can easily recall their names and circumstances.

Some parts of the Catechism will offer more than one prayer or specific prayers, based on a person's circumstances. For instance, under the Fourth Commandment, there are prayers for children who are not yet grown and prayers for those who are grown and caring for their aging parents. Under the Sixth Commandment, there are prayers for those who are single and those who are married. Use whichever words are appropriate to your circumstances.

The First Commandment

You shall have no other gods.

What does this mean? We should fear, love, and trust in God above all things.

Most gracious Triune God, You have revealed Yourself to me in Three Persons who are each truly God, and yet there are not three gods but one God. Father, You have made all things; Lord Jesus, You, the Son, have taken on human flesh in obedience to the Father's will that You save all sinners; O Holy Spirit, You call, gather, enlighten, and sanctify me by the holy Means of Grace, bringing me into the holy faith of Christ for my salvation and delivering to me all of His good gifts. All praise, honor and glory be to You, Father, Son, and Holy Spirit, for You have created me, redeemed me, and sanctify me now and forever.

Teach me, gracious Lord, to fear, love, and trust in nothing more than You. Teach me that because You have done all things for me, I need never look to anything or anyone else for my good but You. Forgive me when I fill my life with so many other things that I fear, love, or trust in more than You, so many idols and false gods.

Father, teach me to trust in Your gracious giving to me of what I need each day for my body and life. Let it be, Father, that I never fear want or need, and may it be that I do not turn away from You because I have so much. Stir up my heart to love You as my Father, because You have loved me in Your Son, Jesus Christ, and continue to love me and provide for me. Above all, let me trust in You for every good gift. Grant that all those who are in trouble or need especially *(names)* may be so kept by Your grace that their trust in You would never fail. Holy Spirit, by my Baptism, the Holy Gospel, the words of Absolution, and Jesus' Body and Blood, keep me in the true faith, keep me in Christ, keep me as a dear child of the Father.

I ask this all, most Blessed Trinity, in and through the Name of the eternal Son, Jesus Christ, my Lord. Amen.

The Second Commandment

You shall not misuse the name of the LORD your God.

What does this mean? We should fear and love God so that we do not curse, swear, use satanic arts, lie, or deceive by His name, but call upon it in every trouble, pray, praise, and give thanks.

Lord Jesus Christ, You have given me Your holy Name to use and call upon in every need, and in and through it I come boldly to the Father. Grant me, by the Holy Spirit, to learn to know Your Name as my greatest treasure and gift, and to use it rightly, calling upon You in every need and giving You thanks always for all things.

Forgive me when I despise Your Name. I often use Your Name wrongly, even as a curse word like it were just a common thing. More than that, I sin against Your holy Commandment by not praying and calling upon You as You have commanded. I have failed to put Your Name upon my lips and my prayers into Your ears. Forgive me for neglecting to use Your Name as You have given me to do.

Now, Lord, hear my prayer. Hear my cry to You for every trouble. Be with those who are in any trouble or are suffering. Especially I call upon Your Name for *(names and circumstances)*. Grant to each of them Your grace and mercy to comfort them and help them to bear their cross. Lord, teach them also to take Your Name boldly upon their lips, to cry out to You in their need, and to call upon You in every trouble.

I praise and thank You, Lord Jesus, that, in Your becoming flesh and taking upon Yourself a human name, You remind me always by that name that You are my Savior, for Your name indeed means, "The LORD saves." What a treasure I have in this Name above all names by which I hear the Good News of what You have done for me at the cross and also by which I approach the throne of grace, asking all things in boldness and confidence. Hear my prayers, for it is in Your Name, the most holy Name of Jesus, that I pray. Amen.

The Third Commandment

Remember the Sabbath day by keeping it holy.

What does this mean? We should fear and love God so that we do not despise preaching and His Word, but hold it sacred and gladly hear and learn it.

What greater gift have You given me, O Father, besides Your Name than Your Word? In the Holy Scriptures and in the faithful preaching of those Scriptures, You teach me my sin and call me to repentance. More than that, You comfort me with the promise that my sins are forgiven for the sake of Jesus Christ, Your Son, who is the Word-become-flesh.

Forgive me, Lord, for despising so great a gift. Here, more than Your saints of old, I have in abundance the written Scriptures. Yet I do not read or study them as I should. In worship, my ears are filled with Your Word, and yet I pay so little attention and am so easily distracted from what I am hearing. Forgive me for such sins and teach me to honor and cherish Your Word as my highest joy and treasure.

(FOR PASTORS)

Father, forgive me for not studying Your Word as I should and not being eager to preach it. You have called me to this Office of the Holy Ministry that by my lips You would preach and teach and proclaim Your Word. Teach me not to despise this Office but with all seriousness to apply myself to learning Your Word, studying my languages, and searching the Scriptures. Grant me the Spirit of Wisdom that I may learn rightly to divide Your Law and Gospel, and to apply each to hardened and repentant sinners in the measure that they need them. In all that I say and do, let me display such joy as an example to others to delight in Your Word. Guard me from false doctrines and wrong preaching. Let my own notions and ideas have no place in my preaching and teaching but let my words always be faithful to what You teach in Your holy Word.

Forgive me, Lord, for neglecting the many opportunities I have to hear and learn Your Word. Forgive me for every worthless excuse I make for neglecting Bible Study, the Divine Service, and any other opportunity to hear Your Word. Forgive me for not listening and learning when my pastors preach. Forgive me also when I do not support and care for my pastors so that they can preach and teach me without worry and concern for their own welfare.

Open my heart, Lord, to hear and believe Your Word. Teach me to read and hear Your Holy Scriptures, seeking only Jesus. Turn me away from any false preaching and teaching that does not comfort me against my sins with the happy news of my forgiveness in Jesus Christ. Turn me away from all fads and religion that seek to teach me something other than what You would deliver to me through my pastors. All praise be to you, Father, for giving me Your holy Word and, by that Word, saving me from my sins and bestowing upon me the gift of eternal life.

+   +   +

Heavenly Father, Your Word is my life. You have taught me that I do not live by bread alone but by every word that proceeds from Your mouth. Therefore, open my ears and heart to hear and believe Your Word. I give You thanks for all the ways that Word comes to me: by the Scriptures, by my pastor's preaching, teaching, and absolving, by water in Baptism, and by the bread and wine that give me the Body and Blood of Jesus. By that very Word, destroy in me the desires of the sinful nature that would despise Your Word. Rather, strengthen the New Man who gladly hears and learns it. May Your Word be a comfort to all Your people and especially *(names)* in their troubles. I ask all of this in and through Jesus Christ, who is the Word-made-flesh and in whom I have all comfort and salvation. Amen.

The Fourth Commandment

Honor your father and your mother.

What does this mean? We should fear and love God so that we do not despise or anger our parents and other authorities, but honor them, serve and obey them, love and cherish them.s

O God, whom in Christ, I call my dear Father, and who through Holy Baptism has made the Church my Mother, hear my prayer for the sake of Your perfect and obedient Son, Jesus. Father, next to Yourself, You have put my parents. They are the ones through whom You gave me life and take care of me. It is to them that You gave the responsibility of raising me and caring for me, and it is to them I owe my love and honor. Forgive me, Father, for every sin against my earthly fathers and mothers. Forgive me for despising my parents and desiring to have parents other than the ones You have given. Teach me to honor and love my parents and so give honor and love to You.

(For Those Who Still Live Under Their Parents)

Father, I plead, by the blood of Your Son, Jesus Christ, that You would wipe away every sin of mine against my mother and father. Stir up in my New Man, by Your Holy Spirit, a desire to be obedient to my parents in all things. When I am troubled, teach me to ask for their advice and seek their wisdom. When they seem to me to be foolish or embarrassing, let not my fear of what others think hinder me from doing my duty of honoring and loving them.

Heavenly Father, I am young and do not know everything. I do not know the struggles my parents face to provide for me and for my family, nor do I know the challenges they may face in their jobs and dealings with others. Therefore, I pray that You would be with my parents in their jobs and in their daily work. I pray that You would keep them from sin and bless them in all that they do. Teach me, O Lord, how I may be a blessing to them and not a burden. As hard as I may think it to be, teach me to submit to their authority and wisdom. Grant me, heavenly Father, to always love and cherish them, seeing my parents as a gift from you, no matter how old I am.

(FOR THOSE WHOSE PARENTS ARE AGING)

Father, my times and days are in Your hands. Teach me to number my days aright that I may know the heart of wisdom. Father, as my parents age, and need more help and care, help me to remember all that they have done for me and that the honor You command me to give them does not cease because I am no longer living in their house. Lord, when my parents are ill or have any need, teach me the patience and wisdom to care for them. Grant me whatever resources I need to make sure that they are not neglected or abandoned in their old age or need. In the last years of their lives, open my heart to extend to them this last duty of honor and love by doing whatever I am able to see that they are cared for and comfortable. Forgive my impatience and desire to avoid my responsibility. Crucify such sinful thoughts within me! Raise me up, by the power of my Baptism, to be a faithful caregiver to those who have raised and cared for me.

(FOR THOSE WHOSE PARENTS ARE DIVORCED)

Father, it is not Your will that the marriage of a man and woman be torn apart, yet now my father and mother are no longer one. Forgive them, Lord, for Jesus' sake, whatever sins caused this terrible breaking apart of their marriage. If it be possible, let them reconcile and be joined again in marriage, and, if that is no longer possible, let them learn to be civil and Christian toward one another. Grant me patience, Father, to love my parents even when the circumstances of their divorce cause me grief and pain. Let neither they nor me play favorites or "take sides." Teach my parents to love their children no less because of a divorce and teach me, their child, not to love them less for their no longer being together. In all things, let me live in the grace and forgiveness You have given me in Jesus Christ.

Gracious Father, through my baptism into Jesus Christ, You have made me Your child in a glorious adoption, making me, who had no heavenly Father, Your own child in Jesus Christ, Your Son. Father, look in mercy upon me in my sadness because my *(father/mother/parents* has/have) left me. By the comfort of the Holy Spirit, relieve the pain I suffer from those You have given to love and care for me but who have neglected their calling. I pray, Father, that wherever they are, You would draw them to Your Word and to repentance and faith. When I sorrow over the loss of my *(father/mother/parents)*, then comfort me with the knowledge that You, my Heavenly Father, will never leave me nor forsake me.

(FOR PARENTS)

Father, You have made me a *(father/mother)* by the gift of children. Grant that I would never use Your holy Commandment as a way to command obedience for its own sake. Rather, teach me by Your Word and Spirit to love and cherish my children and never to grieve or exasperate them. When I am too harsh with them, forgive me, and also teach me to admit my wrong to them and ask their forgiveness. Protect them in all things every day and grant me the wisdom to train them up in the way that they should go, so that when they are old they will not depart from it. Above all, make me to teach them the holy faith of Christ and keep me in that holy faith until I die.

+   +   +

Not only my parents, Lord, but all authority is given by You for my good. Guide and bless all those who are in authority over me: especially teachers and pastors, firefighters and police, mayor and city council, state governor and legislature, President and Congress, all judges and law enforcement officials, and all those whose job it is to protect and care for me outside of my family. Grant them strength to carry out their duties faithfully for the good of those they serve.

Finally, dear Father in heaven, be with those who are sick and suffering or in danger or need, especially *(names)*. For those who are young, grant their parents the wisdom and resources to help them; for those who are older, grant that their children faithfully assist them. In every cross that they bear, let them never forget Your Fatherly love to them in Jesus Christ, that they may rest in the comfort of Your loving arms. I ask this all, dear Father in heaven, for the sake of Jesus Christ, my Lord, in and through whom I am Your dear child and You are my dear Father. Amen.

The Fifth Commandment

You shall not murder.

What does this mean? We should fear and love God so that we do not hurt or harm our neighbor in his body, but help and support him in every physical need.

Lord Jesus Christ, who was murdered at the hands of evil men, yet by that death has blotted out my sins, hear my prayer as I meditate upon the words of Your Commandment. First of all, Lord, grant me, by Your Word and Spirit, such a spirit of patience and peace that I am never stirred up to such anger or hatred against another person that I would hurt them.

Yet You know my sinful heart, Lord Jesus. And You know that even if I do not physically hurt others, I am still a murderer according to Your Law. For You Yourself teach that I should not be angry without a cause and have hatred toward another person. You know my heart and mind. You know the evil thoughts I have had toward others, and You know the words that I have thought of saying and have even spoken aloud. But as you, Lord Jesus, took the place of a murderer, Barabbas, who was set free, so also, by my Baptism into Your name, You have set me free from the condemnation I have deserved.

Gracious Lord, there are many opportunities to help others in need that I have neglected. Whether it be someone in my own family or related to my job or calling, I am easily tempted to keep what is mine for myself out of selfishness when I might have shared it with someone who is in need. For such selfishness, Lord, I ask Your forgiveness. Now teach me, by Your Holy Spirit, to look with compassion upon others and share with those in need whatever I am able, so that I might learn to gladly support my neighbor in every physical need. Before Your throne of grace I now remember those who are in need, especially *(names)*. If there is any physical need I might help supply them in their suffering or difficulty, then let me do so with a selfless and joyful heart.

Lord Jesus Christ, You were once an infant in the womb of Mary. Therefore, let me never condone or support the murder of the unborn which happens so easily and frequently. If I have the opportunity, let me not condemn anyone who has undergone an abortion but, again, provide what I can to help and support them. Forgive those who have been led by evil advice to kill their unborn children. And bring all involved in such decisions to repentance and faith. Likewise, O Lord, teach me that my times are in Your hands so that when I am old or with those who are suffering, I would not turn to any sort of "mercy killing," which is just another word for murder. Let it not be, Lord, that I take part in my society and culture's murderous attitude. Rather, by my words and actions, let me be a witness for life and a support to all who suffer.

Finally, Lord Jesus, look with mercy and blessing upon those whose callings require them to take the life of another, especially those who perform capital punishment, and also soldiers and law enforcement officers who may be required to kill. Grant them peace of mind, knowing that in the kingdom of this world You have permitted such use of force. Bestow upon them the knowledge that by Your death all sins are covered, and let them carry out their callings faithfully and without abusing their authority or power.

Teach me, Lord Jesus Christ, by Your Word, to love others as myself and thereby avoid murderous thoughts, words, and actions. I rejoice in the forgiveness You have won by trading places with me and setting me free by the forgiveness of sins You won for me on the cross. Dearest Jesus, hear my prayers offered up in Your Name. Amen.

The Sixth Commandment

You shall not commit adultery.

What does this mean? We should fear and love God so that we lead a sexually pure and decent life in what we say and do, and husband and wife love and honor each other.

Most gracious heavenly Father, in the Garden of Eden You established the holy state of marriage when You presented Adam with a bride from his own side. At the death of Your Son, by blood and water, You brought forth His bride, the holy Christian Church which is born and sustained by the washing of Holy Baptism and the food of Christ's Holy Supper. Therefore, teach me to regard holy marriage as a sacred and serious institution. Teach me never to take it lightly, even though the world despises it and perverts sexuality into something self-centered. Father, it is Your gift for a man and woman to be united in marriage to share their life together, to be a comfort and support for one another, and, as You see fit, to bring from their union the gift of children. Lord, forgive me for despising marriage, for thinking about sexuality in the way of the world, for not standing up for this holy institution, and, most of all, for neglecting to see in marriage the holy picture of Christ and His Church. Father, forgive me for all of those sins against Your Sixth Commandment. Also, I pray for all those who are wrapped up in sins against marriage and who have fallen into fornication and adultery. Forgive those who have despised marriage and live together as if they are married but are not. Bring repentance and faith to those who have fallen into twisted and unnatural lifestyles which dishonor marriage and deny the truth of that picture of Christ and His Church. Especially, I ask this for *(names)*. In all things, let me never be judgmental but, rejoicing in the forgiveness of Christ, enable me to bear witness to the truth and the beauty of Your will for marriage.

(FOR THOSE WHO ARE SINGLE)

Father, if it be Your will, give to me that person with whom I might spend my life in the blessed state of marriage. In my dating, teach me to be courteous and caring, respectful and loving. Guard me by Your Word and Spirit from the temptations with which the devil, world, and flesh assault me. Guard my lips and my heart that I may not speak or act from lust but in chastity and patience. Protect me and those I date from engaging in such behavior and activity as is only proper for a husband and wife. Teach me to guard and preserve my honor and reputation. If it be Your will, bring me together in holy marriage, and may I be chaste in all that I say and do until that day. Heavenly Father, as long as I am not married, teach me purity in thoughts, words, and actions, so that I may bring no dishonor to Christ or His Name that I bear. Guard me from all temptations of the flesh which seek to pervert my view of the opposite sex and destroy my appreciation and esteem of marriage. Father, You know that I am surrounded by so many opportunities for sin in what my eyes see and my ears hear and my heart thinks about. Therefore, as Your servant, the psalmist, said, so I ask You, "Turn away my eyes from beholding worthless things and revive me in Your Way" (Psalm 119:37). For all of my sins against this holy Commandment, let the blood of my holy Bridegroom, Jesus, cleanse me and teach me to rejoice and await His coming with holy joy and anticipation.

(FOR THOSE WHO ARE MARRIED)

Father, You have given to me the gift of a spouse. Teach me to repent of all selfishness and to give myself wholly and completely to *(name, my wife/husband)*. I pray that You would protect us both from all temptations to stray outside the bonds of holy marriage. Teach me to honor the vows which I made in Your sight. Teach us to love and cherish one another as Your holy Commandment instructs us. Teach husbands to love their wives as Christ loved His Church and wives to submit to their husbands as the Church submits to Christ's care and authority. In all things, drive from me all selfishness and self-centeredness. Teach me, Father, to hold my tongue from saying things that would hurt my spouse or make my spouse look bad to others. By Your Word and Spirit, instruct my lips to say only those things to and about my spouse that demonstrate a godly love and affection for him/her. I thank you, Father, for the joy of this union of marriage. I thank You for the companion You have given me, the physical relationship, and the emotional and practical support that we offer to one another. Forgive me for despising my marriage and for falling into patterns of selfishness and putting myself ahead of my spouse. With great joy, teach us together as husband and wife to love and honor each other and to joyfully await together the coming of our Lord Jesus to gather us for the eternal wedding feast.

+   +   +

Gracious Lord, all around me marriage is despised and looked down upon and attacked. Teach me as a Christian to give a faithful and godly witness to marriage not only as the foundation of all families and society but, above all, as the picture of Christ and His love for the Church. Father, there are many whose marriages have fallen into trouble and many that have ended in divorce. There are many godly marriages which need to be strengthened. Hear my prayer for all those who are married, whose marriages are in trouble or who have suffered the breakup of their marriages, and those whose spouses have died and now struggle with bitter loneliness, especially *(names)*. Strengthen them by the forgiveness of sins given in Your holy Means of Grace. Strengthen them by Christ's love for His Bride, the Church, that they may faithfully love and honor each other. In all things, let all Your people, whether married or single, lead sexually pure and decent lives in what they say and do, so that Your Name may be glorified and the witness of Christ and His Church may be plain for all the world to see. I ask this, heavenly Father, for the sake of the holy Bridegroom, even Jesus Christ, my Lord. Amen.

The Seventh Commandment

You shall not steal.

What does this mean? We should fear and love God so that we do not take our neighbor's money or possessions, or get them in any dishonest way, but help him to improve and protect his possessions and income.

Heavenly Father, all that I have is a gift from Your hand. Teach me to be thankful for whatever You give me, and guard me from jealousy and covetousness for what others have been given. Teach me, Father, to receive my earthly blessings, my possessions and property, with thanksgiving and contentedness. In this way, O Lord, I will learn to be happy with what I am given and not take away what You have given to others, steal from them, cheat them, or defraud them of their possessions and property.

Forgive me, Father, for Jesus' sake, for all my sins against Your Seventh Commandment. Forgive me for having taken from others what does not belong to me. Grant me the honesty and conviction to confess my stealing to anyone from whom I've taken anything and to give back, pay back, or do whatever must be done to make things right again. By Your Spirit, teach me the full extent of what stealing is, so that I am not puffed up and made arrogant just because I have never shoplifted or committed an actual crime. Teach me, Father, that to take anything that should be paid for but is not is to steal from others. Whether it is big or small, if I should give a fair price to whomever it belongs, let me do so.

Lord, there are so many temptations to be dishonest and to steal. There is cheating at school, falsifying documents, cheating on my taxes, claiming credit for work that others have done, getting paid for work that I did not do, wasting time when I am "on the clock," giving away or receiving papers, work, books, music, or whatever else that I have not rightly paid for, and there are so many other temptations and ways to steal! I am surrounded by the devil, the world, and my flesh who would cause me to lie and cheat and steal to my own advantage and to the hurt of others.

Protect me from these enemies, Lord, by the holy Means of Grace in which You forgive and strengthen me!

Teach me also, Father, to help my neighbor improve and protect his possessions and income. Wherever I have the opportunity to restore to another person what they have lost or what has been taken, grant me the charity to do so. When others have lost their earthly possessions or had them taken from them, make me generous with mine so that I may serve my neighbor by supplying what they need from the abundance of what You have given me. Forgive my stinginess and let me never withhold what I am able to give, so that I may serve my neighbor and care for them.

Also, Lord, I pray about another kind of stealing, which Your Word calls "robbing God." That is, Father, my lack of offerings. Open my heart and hand so that I may not give leftovers and a thoughtless contribution, but a generous and faithful tithe and offering from my resources. Forgive me, Lord, when my offerings have been thoughtless and sinful in Your sight. Teach me that my contribution to the congregation is not for Your sake—You don't need my money!—but for the sake of my pastor, that he and his family may live without worry, for the sake of my brothers and sisters in Christ, whom my offering helps care for and serve, and for the maintenance of my church and its property, that we may always have a place to worship and receive Your holy gifts!

Finally, dear Father, teach me to have the same humility which was in Christ, that He did not consider His being God something to be taken like a robbery but rather submitted Himself to the cross and death for my sake. I thank You that, for the sake of all sinners, my Lord was hung between two thieves, and that He gave the gift of paradise to the thief who looked to Him for salvation. So I look to Christ, dear Father, and ask Your forgiveness and salvation for His sake. Be with all those who are in need or in trouble, especially *(names)*. When it comes to their possessions and property, grant them whatever they need to be taken care of and relieved of their suffering. Make me generous in sharing what You have given me with them, in order to help and support them. I ask all these things, heavenly Father, in the Name of Jesus Christ, Your Son, whom You have given to me as my holy and saving possession far beyond all earthly treasure, and through whom I have an inheritance kept in heaven that will never perish, spoil, or fade. Amen.

The Eighth Commandment

You shall not give false testimony against your neighbor.

What does this mean? We should fear and love God so that we do not tell lies about our neighbor, betray him, slander him, or hurt his reputation, but defend him, speak well of him, and explain everything in the kindest way.

Lord Jesus, put on trial by the words of false witnesses, purge from me every sinful desire to speak and say things that will harm others. It is because of Your death and resurrection that what God the Father says about me now is not the truth of my condemnation for sin, but it is the truth of my righteousness in You. Therefore, Lord Jesus, teach me to speak always and only in ways that build others up and explain things in the kindest way.

Lord Jesus, my tongue is like a spark that causes great wildfires! With but a few words I can cause misery and sadness for others by what I say. How easy it is to speak badly of my friends or spouse or family or any other people so that I might be built up and they might be torn down. How easy it is to take what I know about others, good or bad, and turn it into gossip or tattling or slander. How much Lord, I enjoy speaking badly about others while becoming angry when others speak badly about me! How easily I speak about others in a way that lowers them in the sight of those who hear what I say, and then I defend my actions by saying, "But it's true!" How often I grumble and complain about others and call it "venting" rather than what it is: sin against Your holy Commandment of speaking about others. For all of these and every sin against this Commandment, I beg Your forgiveness, that by the blood You shed on Calvary, my evil and sinful words would be blotted out.

Lord grant me Your Holy Spirit by Your Word so that I may learn to speak only those things which build up and do not tear down. Teach me to put away all lying and false talk. Stir up in me the ability to speak well of others and explain their actions in a good way. Teach me to look at others and speak about them in a way that reflects the truth that they also are ones for whom You died. It is so terribly easy, Lord, to jump to conclusions, to assume the worst about someone, and to strike out quickly with harsh words either to their face or behind their back. When such a temptation comes upon me to act this way, bury it in Your wounds and give me Your Holy Spirit to shut the mouth of my sinful nature and bring no harm to others by my words.

Lord Jesus, teach me the Christian art of knowing when to speak the truth in love and when to hold my tongue. Grant me that I never break a confidence I am to keep nor speak the truth in such a way that it would bring harm to someone or hurt their reputation. As You speak of me, not as sinner but as holy in Your Father's sight, so let me speak of others in this way and explain the actions of my neighbor in a holy manner which does not hurt them but builds up their reputation in the eyes of those who hear me talk.

Most especially Lord, teach me in my words to overlook whatever someone may do against me. To explain everything in the kindest way or to put the best construction on things is impossible, Lord, without Your Word and Spirit. Left to myself, I should only ever jump on those who do something against me, mock and speak hatefully of those I do not like, and puff myself up by tearing others down! Forgive me for having done so! As Noah's faithful sons walked backward to cover up his drunken nakedness, so teach me to do likewise with my words, to cover up and put up with and ignore the faults of others. Teach me that skill of speaking about other people in the way that I wish they would speak of me.

Lord, it may be that I am called to give a witness to something in court or in some other official capacity. When such a calling is given to me, guard me from every temptation to lie or give false testimony. Rather let me faithfully recount the truth as I am called to do in such a situation. When I must give an account of Your Word and faith, let me do so in truth without lying or shying away from Your Word. Teach me also Lord, by Your Holy Spirit, to know right preaching and teaching from Your Word and to turn away from and despise any preaching or teaching which is done falsely and wrongly in Your Name.

Gracious Lord, there are many sick and suffering around me and many others who have troubles of various kinds. I remember here *(names)*. When I speak about them, keep me from belittling them, criticizing them, or saying anything against whatever weakness or trouble they suffer. Rather, let my words about them be positive and let my words to them be comforting and helpful. Let me always direct them to You and to Your promises and Means of Grace. Gracious Lord, my mouth is so easily given over to the service of sinfulness. Therefore, I pray with the psalmist that You cleanse my tongue and speech! "O Lord, open my lips. And my mouth will declare Your praise." Let it be so, Lord Jesus, for the sake of Your holy Name which was spoken upon me at my Baptism and which cleanses me from all my sins. Amen.

The Ninth Commandment

You shall not covet your neighbor's house.

What does this mean? We should fear and love God so that we do not scheme to get our neighbor's inheritance or house, or get it in a way which only appears right, but help and be of service to him in keeping it.

Heavenly Father, now in the Ninth Commandment, You teach me the gift of contentment. Since You have graciously given me all that I need for this body and life, teach me to be content with the things that You have given me. Rescue me from the worldly lust of always wanting more and more and never seeming to have enough. The world teaches greed to my flesh: "Buy more. Get more. Have it now. Pay later." Through my Baptism into Christ, rescue me from such lusting after whatever the world says I can't live without. Teach me that man truly does not live by bread alone but by every word that comes from Your mouth.

Father, You know my coveting. You know my daydreaming about the things that I do not have. You see how thinking about things that You have not given me distracts me from my daily callings, my job, my caring for others. You see how even with my close friends and relatives I try to think up ways to get from them what is theirs. Father, by the blood of Jesus, who was content to do Your will and die for my sins, cleanse me from all covetousness and the desire to sin against others by coveting what is theirs. Forgive my envy and jealousy toward others and what they have. Whenever I am tempted to look longingly at the things of this world, grant that the Holy Spirit would pull me back into the comfort and contentment of Your Word and Gifts, and the blessings which You have already given to me.

Lord, it is easy to take advantage of other people. Even my laws permit me to profit from the misfortune of others. Quench my greed to snap up what belongs to someone else simply because I stand to benefit from their failure or misfortune. Call me to repentance from any work or project whose goal is to take something from another person only because they cannot afford to keep it or because I can claim some legal right that allows them to lose it. Such actions are not loving and caring for my neighbor but rather harm them.

Instead, when I have the opportunity and the means, stir up my heart to assist those in need and to help others keep and improve their inheritance and property. Lord, keep me from doing any harm against another person's property and instead take whatever steps I can to help them maintain what is theirs. Teach me respect for the property and belongings of others and to care for whatever belongs to my family and friends and neighbors with the same care I would want shown for my own possessions. Guard me from all temptations to vandalize, destroy, ruin, steal, or otherwise wreck the earthly goods You have given to others. Rather, enable me to help clean, restore, and maintain what belongs to those around me. As You have given me true contentment, keep away from me all lures of the evil one not to be content but instead restless and covetous.

Lord, help those who are suffering and in need, especially *(names)*. Where their inheritance or house or property are in danger, lead me to be helpful in whatever way I can. In the restlessness of their misery, grant them true faith and contentment in Jesus. Whenever I see the things of this world passing away, encourage me and them with Your promise that Your Word never passes away, and therefore nothing can take from us our greatest treasure and inheritance, our eternal life in Jesus Christ.

In Holy Baptism, You have given me a washing of rebirth and renewal in the Holy Spirit, You have poured out the Spirit generously on me, justified me with Your grace, and made me an heir of eternal life. With such an eternal inheritance awaiting me, kept in heaven from perishing and spoiling, so let me enjoy the things of this life without clinging to them as idols. I give You thanks for all that You have given to me but most especially for the treasure You Yourself have prepared for me in heaven. Let that treasure, even Jesus Christ my Lord, be my true contentment in all circumstances. I ask it for the sake of that which is more precious than gold, the very blood of Jesus Himself, in His Name I pray. Amen.

The Tenth Commandment

You shall not covet your neighbor's wife, or his manservant or maidservant, his ox or donkey, or anything that belongs to your neighbor.

What does this mean? We should fear and love God so that we do not entice or force away our neighbor's wife, workers, or animals, or turn them against him, but urge them to stay and do their duty.

Heavenly Father, Giver of every good gift, my prayer today is that, just as You rescue and protect me from coveting my neighbor's possessions, so also deliver me from the evil of coveting the people that You have given to my neighbor. In a world that teaches me to do whatever I want, there is a horrible and deadly temptation to covet the people that You have not given me. I covet and desire the spouse of another person instead of the spouse or chaste life You have given to me. I covet and desire someone else's parents or children, instead of the families that You have given to me. I long for a different boss or employees. I am jealous of the friends that other people have. In so many ways, the devil, the world, and my sinful nature set me up to lust after other people, those whom You have not given me in one way or another.

For all such sin, forgive me! Blot out by the blood of the Lamb my lusting after others and my coveting of persons. When such temptations come upon me, check and hinder me by the Holy Spirit through Your Word and Gifts. Open my eyes that I may see any inappropriateness in my actions toward others. Teach me, by this Commandment, to recognize the subtle ways this sin begins in my heart until it is stirred up with affections toward others so much that I would wish that person was mine rather than my neighbor's.

Father, let me learn from this Commandment how I should live. Teach me never to become such a friend or make such confidences or spend so much time with another person's spouse or children or parents or whomever, that their friendship with me weakens and destroys the relationships that You have already given them. When I am married, guard me that I never give to another person the trust and confidence and intimacy that belongs only to my own spouse. Keep me from ignoring my own parents by giving to someone else's parents the respect and honor that are due to my own. When I am among my friends, do not let me manipulate them so that I am raised up in their sight and others are lowered. Let it be that I do not seek to take a friend from another person or act in such a way that they are forced to choose between friendship with me or someone else. In short, Lord, work in me by Your Holy Spirit, through Your Word and Sacraments, so that I do not fall into the trap of turning away from the people You have given me in my life to seek comfort and advice and friendship and love from those whom You have not given me in those ways!

Now, Lord, having asked for protection against these sins for myself, I pray that You would make me a faithful Christian toward my friends and neighbors. When I see a marriage in trouble, teach me the wisdom to point that husband and wife to Your promises, Your forgiveness, and Your will that they remain married and grow in that marriage. When friends complain about other friends or parents or bosses or whomever, give me the wisdom to guide them away from talk which tears down and instead urge them to "stay and do their duty," that is, to love and honor and respect and work diligently for the people You have given them in their lives. Whenever You give me the opportunity to witness to Your love, in forgiving hurting sinners and restoring them to each other, make me to do so. With Your holy Word, therefore, guard me against coveting the persons of others while at the same time making me faithfully support and help others in those situations.

Lord, have mercy upon all those who are sick or suffering or in any kind of need. Hear my prayer especially for *(names)* and their spouses, children, parents, friends, and loved ones. In their trials, there are great opportunities for sinning against this very Commandment, both for myself and for their loved ones. Guard my heart and mind from every evil suggestion and temptation to take advantage of them in their weakness or to steal away from them the people they need to support them. When those whom You have given to be there for them grow weak and weary with their responsibilities, make me a faithful witness to remind them of their duty and calling to serve. Most of all, make me a faithful witness to Your faithfulness and love in Jesus Christ, that they may be recalled to their duty by Your promise never to leave them or forsake them. Hear all of these prayers, merciful Father, in and through the Name of Jesus Christ, Your Son, my Lord. Amen.

The Close of the Commandments

What does God say about all these commandments?

> He says, "I, the LORD your God, am a jealous God, punishing the children for the sin of the fathers to the third and fourth generation of those who hate Me, but showing love to a thousand generations of those who love Me and keep My commandments." (Ex. 20: 5–6)

> *What does this mean? God threatens to punish all who break these commandments. Therefore, we should fear His wrath and not do anything against them. But He promises grace and every blessing to all who keep these commandments. Therefore, we should also love and trust in Him and gladly do what He commands.*

Lord God, heavenly Father, You have given me Your holy Commandments as a list of Your blessings and Your instructions on how I should live and receive those blessings, and protect them for others. The Commandments teach me how to live, how to glorify You in my actions, and how You desire me to serve others. These Commandments teach me what is the happy life, living under Your Fatherly care, protection, and guidance. Your teaching and instruction is for me a holy food, sweeter than honey, and more precious than gold and jewels! Yet because of my sin, Your holy Law has become for me a judging mirror that exposes my sins and shows me that I do not love You or my neighbor as I ought to do. Even worse than heaping upon me the true and just guilt of my sins, Your Word shows that I am condemned for breaking these Commandments, and that no one is without sin. Yes, Lord, through and through, by every Commandment, I am crushed by the mighty blow of Your hammer and brought down to the very depths of hell.

Here Lord, I confess to You that I do not fear, love, and trust in You above all things. I have learned, by meditating on these holy Commandments, that I am an idolater, someone who misuses Your name, and a despiser of Your Word. I have not honored my parents and other authorities, nor kept myself from hurting others. I have despised marriage and chastity, and I am quick to try to get what does not belong to me. I so easily tear down the reputations of others, and, above all, I am not content with what You have given me. I deserve, as Your Law says, Your holy and everlasting punishment.

If that were all there is, O Lord, You would still be righteous and holy and just in my condemnation. Yet with You there is forgiveness, therefore You are feared! For You sent Your only -begotten Son into the flesh. Now Jesus has come and taken the Law upon Himself. He has lived it perfectly, spotlessly, without sin. At every turn, my Lord has kept the Commandments, never breaking one. Not only that, but He has taken upon Himself my sins and my guilt. He was made sin for me, and He became the curse for me so that all my sin is laid upon Him, the spotless Lamb. And by His death He has taken that sin away. Your Son, dear Father, has lived my life as I should have and has died the death I deserved. By His resurrection from the dead, by my Baptism into Him, by the preaching of Your Word, by the Absolution, and by His Body and Blood given me to eat and drink—by all these Gifts, You have made what is mine His, my sins, and what is His mine, everlasting righteousness, innocence, and blessedness. For this, Father, accept my grateful praise and thanksgiving!

Now, cleansed by the blood of Christ and filled with the Holy Spirit, teach me true fear, love, and trust in You, O God. Teach me truly and rightly to fear my sins and Your wrath. Let me be afraid of Your judgment so that I am kept from sinning. Yet let me also love You and trust in You, knowing that because my sins are forgiven in Christ, I am freed from trying to save myself. Teach me, Lord, that the works that Christ does in and through me according to Your Commandments are not done to make me right with you. Jesus has done that! Teach me, rather, that my works are done and Your Commandments kept for the sake of Your glory and my neighbor's welfare and service. Teach me to do joyfully all that You have commanded so that I may learn to receive the gifts that You have given to me and to serve my neighbor by helping preserve and protect what You have given to them.

Father, if I should look to myself for the strength to keep Your Law, I would instantly fail. Therefore, let me never trust in myself but in Christ who lives in me and who through me accomplishes good things according to Your Commandments. Behold in their weakness, all those who are in need, especially *(names)*. Forgive them, too, by the blood of Christ, for any failure to fear, love, and trust in You when they suffer. By the same grace which is given to all Your people in Your Gospel and Sacraments, strengthen them truly to fear you, to love You, and to trust in You, so that they will not be brought by temptation into unbelief and despair. In all things, whatsoever they suffer, do not let their hope in You fail, and do not forsake them in their struggles.

Apart from Christ, dear Father, Your Law counts me as a sinner who is under Your judgment. But in Jesus Christ, I am Your forgiven and perfect child, clothed with the holiness of Jesus. For His sake You have forgotten my sins. Give me Your Holy Spirit, by Your Word, so that I may always delight in Your will and walk in Your ways. Write Your Law upon my heart so that I may, with joy and new life in Christ, rejoice to live as You would have me live. Through Christ living in me, work in me both to will and to do those things which glorify You and serve my neighbor. This I ask, heavenly Father, for the sake of Jesus Christ, Your Son, my Lord, who lives and reigns with You and the Holy Spirit, one God, now and forever. Amen.

The First Article, Part 1

I believe in God, the Father Almighty, Maker of heaven and earth.

> *What does this mean? I believe that God has made me and all creatures; that He has given me my body and soul, eyes, ears, and all my members, my reason and all my senses, and still takes care of them. For all this it is my duty to thank and praise, serve and obey Him. This is most certainly true.*

I thank You, heavenly Father, through Jesus Christ Your dear Son, that through Him You have made me Your child so that I can call You my Father. I thank You for the gift of my life, bringing me into this world and preserving me unto this day. I thank You that, even in this fallen world, You still see fit to bring life into existence. What sort of God would You be if You could only take what already existed and make something out of it? But you, Father, have made all that there is out of nothing. What sort of God would You be if You just made everything and then stood back and left it to itself? But You, Father, continue in the work of preserving Your creation and rescuing me from the curse on this earth that came because of my disobedience and fall into sin.

In six days You made all that there is. On the seventh day You rested and blessed and made holy that day of rest. I am Your creature and You the Creator. Yet now, Lord, see how the world despises the One who made them. See how we have turned our backs upon Your gracious hand. See how we have ignored the testimony of Your creation, that the heavens declare Your glory, and that the earth shows forth the work of Your hands! Instead, Father, the world denies You and claims its origins from randomness and chance. It makes Your creation of no value and it ascribes no purpose and meaning to life. On the one hand, there are those who deny that You exist, and, on the other, they worship the things You have made. Forgive me, Father, through the blood of Your incarnate Son, for every thought or idea that seeks to ignore Your fatherly care and protection or to make a false god out of things that You have made and given.

Father, let me not take for granted all that You have given me in my life and body: my ability to see and hear, to taste and touch and smell. You have not only made me but have given me the gifts of Your creation so that I might enjoy them. Teach me never to take these gifts for granted and not to use them for my own selfishness but for Your glory and the good of my neighbor. Turn my eyes from looking at worthless things and instead unto beauty and goodness. Guard my ears from wicked words and sounds and let them be filled with Your Word. Set a watch over my mouth, O Lord, and guard the door of my lips, that I may speak nothing to blaspheme You or hurt someone else; rather open my lips that my mouth may declare Your praise. Deliver me from the temptation to use my body for sin and instead put it to use in the service of those around me, that I may be a "little Christ," and do good to others.

Heavenly Father, if, in Your infinite wisdom and fatherly love and mercy, You permit me or someone else to be deprived of these gifts of eyes or ears or health of body, then teach us to accept this from Your Fatherly hand without complaining or bitterness. Rather, let me recall that because Christ is risen, I too shall rise and be made perfect on the Last Day. Teach me also, Father, that through my Baptism into Jesus Christ, I am already perfect in Your sight, and therefore no matter what I suffer, I am Your dear child in Jesus and lack nothing. Father, hear my prayers for those who suffer in their lives and bodies and health, especially *(names)*. When their members and senses fail, let them hold fast to You, and let me use my members and senses to help and assist them. Whatever they must suffer, do not let it become a stumbling block to their confession of Your faithfulness and love, but let them trust all the more in Jesus Christ and the hope and promise of the resurrection in which You will wipe away every tear from their eyes.

Finally, heavenly Father, I know that because of sin and its curse in this world, the time will come when I will pass away. The day of my death will come when my earthly life ends. Teach me, Lord, that, even though death comes, You truly still take care of me. Your Son, who took on flesh and was incarnate, took on Himself my life and also my death. And since

He is risen from the dead and has conquered all sin and death, I too have victory over these things. Therefore, when my life fails and death comes, keep me in the holy faith of Jesus. Fill my ears with Your promises. Remind me of the clothing of my Baptism. Feed my body and soul with the Body and Blood of Jesus. Open my lips to speak the "Amen" to Your will and rejoice in the days of life You have given me. When my last hour comes, open my eyes to the glory that awaits me, and bring me to the eternal life with You that You have promised in Jesus Christ. In life and in death, You have made me and I am Yours, Father. Hear my prayer in the Name of Jesus Christ, my Lord. Amen.

The First Article, Part 2

I believe in God, the Father Almighty, Maker of heaven and earth.

What does this mean? He also gives me clothing and shoes, food and drink, house and home, wife and children, land, animals, and all I have. He richly and daily provides me with all that I need to support this body and life. For all this it is my duty to thank and praise, serve and obey Him. This is most certainly true.

Heavenly Father, from whom comes every good and perfect gift, hear my prayer of thanksgiving for everything You give me to support my body and life. Not only did You create me and still take care of me, You also give me everything I need in this life. My sinful flesh loves to take credit: "What I have I have earned. I worked hard for it. It's mine. I got it for myself." Yet, Lord, were You to withdraw Your gracious hand even for a moment, I would lose everything and perish! Forgive me, Father, when I forget that all I have comes from Your Fatherly hand. Even the means by which I receive my earthly gifts—my job or parents or the help of others— are Your gift and blessing to me.

Father, I thank You for the basic necessities of life which You provide for me: the food and drink that sustains my body; the clothing and shoes by which You cover my nakedness and keep me comfortable; the house and home in which I live and sleep, sheltered and protected from the things which would harm me; my family *(parents who provide for me, husband/ wife and children who make up my family, grandparents, aunts, uncles)*; and my country, government, neighbors, and, of course, all my friends. I thank you, Father, for pets, toys, the tools of my trade, the things that I enjoy as hobbies—everything great or small that You have given to me as a material gift for my enjoyment of Your creation. Let me never neglect to see that all these things come from You and therefore to give You thanks for them.

Forgive me when I despise the gifts that You give me. Especially when I think they are not enough or I lust for and covet something else or different, call me to repentance by Your Word so that I may learn to be content with all that You have given. Forgive me, Father, for getting all wrapped up in the things of this world so that I forget Your goodness and promise to take care of me. Teach me that I really do not live by bread alone but by every word which proceeds from Your mouth. Grant me what I need that I may be satisfied and cared for without worry. Let me not be so rich that I despise You and turn away from You, thinking I do not need You. Yet let me never be so poor that I resort to stealing or worse ways of providing for myself. In all things, let me trust You and seek Your kingdom and in Your grace, add all these things unto me.

Heavenly Father, You know the needs of all Your people. Provide for them what each one needs for their health and support. I ask for Your special care of those who are in particular need, especially *(names)*. If a lack of some material thing causes them suffering, then supply it Lord. And open my heart to a willingness to selflessly share what You have given me if it will help my brothers and sisters who are in need. Trusting in Your never-failing goodness to me, let me never shrink back from helping someone in need.

Finally, heavenly Father, if it seems good to You to allow me to be deprived of some material things, let me not despair but trust in Your goodness to care for me. Teach me, above all, to trust in Christ, the Bread of Life, knowing that in having Him I have all things and that, since I am Your child and have the Holy Spirit, I can never truly suffer poverty or want. As I enjoy the earthly gifts that You give me, help me always to look heavenward to rejoice in the treasure which Christ has stored up for me there, where moth and rust cannot destroy and thieves cannot break in and steal. Preserve me in my body and life in the holy faith of Jesus that I may rejoice to come into my eternal inheritance which never perishes, spoils or fades, kept for me in Jesus Christ. It is in His Name that I offer these prayers. Amen.

The First Article, Part 3

I believe in God, the Father Almighty, Maker of heaven and earth.

> *What does this mean? He defends me against all danger and guards and protects me from all evil. All this He does only out of Fatherly divine goodness and mercy, without any merit or worthiness in me. For all this it is my duty to thank and praise, serve and obey Him. This is most certainly true.*

Heavenly Father, You have rescued me from sin and death by sending Your Son to take away my sins on the cross and to rise again. By His perfect life, the sacrifice of His death, His resurrection and ascension; by my Baptism into Him, by my Absolution from all sins, by the Holy Gospel which preaches Christ, and by His Body and Blood—by all these You have made me Your child, and therefore it is true that nothing in heaven or on earth or under the earth can separate me from Your love, which is in Jesus Christ my Lord. This also means that no matter what I suffer in this life, whether sickness or sadness, tragedy or even death itself, none of it can truly be an evil that can destroy me. This is how You guard and protect me from all evil. Not that I won't suffer such things, but they cannot cause me to perish eternally or undo what Your Son has accomplished for me and bestowed upon me by the Spirit and Your Word and Sacraments.

Therefore, Father, I plead for Your mercy and forgiveness because I so often fail to remember that being in Christ means there is no evil that can harm me. Rather, I worry about so many things that I think are terrible and the end of the world. I worry and fret over money and material things. I suffer sickness and pain as if they are the worst thing ever. I weep and mourn as if death is truly the end. Forgive me, Father, for Jesus' sake, of every doubting time when I have questioned Your goodness because of the evil things I undergo. Forgive me for doubting Your mercy. Above all, forgive me for thinking that such things are some sort of punishment or "lesson" I must learn. Rather, teach me to receive Your Fatherly chastening with trust in Your mercy and Your promise to work all things for the good of those who love you. Teach me, above all, being in Christ, to despise the devil and his temptations to doubt and unbelief. Bring me to a true faith and a glad confession of these Catechism words: that You really do guard and protect me from all evil because I am in Christ.

Forgive me, also, dear Father, for the bold and sinful assumption that what I have is what I have earned. Forgive me for ever thinking that I am somehow worthy of Your love or deserve the things that You have given me. I do not deserve the life You have given, the earthly goods that You provide, or the protection from evil that You promise. Rather, my sinfulness deserves nothing but death. Teach me, by Your Word, to learn that all that You give comes because of Your fatherly divine goodness and mercy. I praise and thank You, heavenly Father, for that divine and fatherly goodness. I thank You that You have revealed this mercy to me in and through Jesus Christ, through whom alone I always know Your heart toward me. Let me never presume to know Your heart and mind toward me, especially on the basis of my life, but let me always seek You in Christ, confident that You love and care for me as He Himself has shown by bringing me to You.

Wherever there is evil that comes upon others, let them also stand fast and unmoved in Christ. Here I remember *(names)* whom particular evils and struggles have overtaken. Guard them, Father, from every temptation to doubt Your goodness, despair of Your mercy, or turn away from Christ. Rather, by Your Word and Sacraments, confirm them in the faith and strengthen them to carry whatever crosses You have allowed them to bear. Teach me, Father, to help them carry their burdens and to remind them with the brotherly encouragement of Christians, that Your love for them in Jesus Christ will never fail.

For everything great and small, seen and unseen that You give and provide for me, I owe You unending thanks and praise, my obedience and service. There is no way to repay You, Father, for all that You have given, so I will not live under the burden of thinking I owe what I cannot pay. Only stir up my heart to a life that is confident of Your mercy, gladly receives

Your Word and Gifts, and joyfully serves others in the ways my callings. Let my life be bound by the law of love by which I might learn, not to save myself by my own works, but that, trusting in Christ, I learn to do works of love and mercy for others, too. There is no God like You, no Father who can equal Your grace and mercy. It is Christ who has shown me You, the Father, and I rejoice to confess You as my true heavenly Father. All thanks and praise to you, Father in heaven, through Jesus Christ, Your Son, my Lord. Amen.

The Second Article, Part 1

And in Jesus Christ, His only Son, our Lord, who was conceived by the Holy Spirit, born of the Virgin Mary, suffered under Pontius Pilate, was crucified, died and was buried. He descended into hell. The third day He rose again from the dead. He ascended into heaven and sits at the right hand of God, the Father Almighty. From thence He will come to judge the living and the dead.

> *What does this mean? I believe that Jesus Christ, true God, begotten of the Father from eternity and also true man, born of the Virgin Mary, is my Lord. This is most certainly true.*

Now, Lord Jesus, my thoughts turn to Your holy incarnation in which You took upon Yourself a human nature in the womb of Mary in order to be as I am, yet without sin, and thereby to suffer and die for my sins to take them away! What mystery! What Wisdom! What mercy! What a thing never heard of before, that God Himself should take on what He has made so that He may save what was made and has fallen! Oh the infinite majesty of the Son who, in obedience to His Father, even though He was rich, became poor for my sake, that by His poverty I might have the riches of God! You, O eternal Son, have become man and taken my sins, becoming sin for me that I might become in You the righteousness of God. You, Lord, became man so that You might be under the curse of the Law, hanging on a tree to redeem me from the curse of the Law. Hear now, Lord Jesus, Son of God, my praise and thanks for what You have done by becoming man!

Lord Jesus, keep always in my mind and heart this truth: that it was not some goodness in me that was worth saving which caused You to come down and become man. Rather, it was the grace and mercy of Your Father who sent You and Your perfect and willing obedience to Him that brought You from the eternal realms of light to this world dark with sin. Forgive me, Lord Jesus, for every vain attempt to explain from myself why You should be so good to me. Rather, teach me to cast myself and my vanity aside, to confess my total and complete sinfulness which, apart from You, would cause me to suffer everlasting punishment and separation from God.

Son of God, You came into this world and took upon Yourself a human nature. By doing so, You lost none of Your Divine glory and majesty, but it was hidden under Your flesh that I may not perish to see it. You gave nothing up of Your Divine nature, and yet Your human nature is full and complete and, above all, to my benefit, pure and free from sin. While I may not grasp with my mind or explain from my senses the mystery of Your incarnation, guard me from ever speaking wrongly about how You have joined Yourself to a human nature and are now one Christ for all eternity. Lord, if it would be that You were somehow not truly God, then Your sacrifice for sins could not save me, for it would be of no value to anyone but You, at the most. Then, Lord, if it would be that You were somehow not truly man, then also You would not have saved me, for You cannot save something that You are not. May all such thoughts perish within me! Therefore, Lord Jesus, teach me by Your Holy Word, given me in the blessed Scriptures, to confess You truly and worship You faithfully.

Lord, when Your holy angel announced to the Virgin Mary that she would bear the Son of God, she responded in faith with her "Amen." Forgive me, Lord, for every instance in which I have despised Your Word and instead desired my own will and to go my own way. Fill my ears, as You did Mary's with Your Word, that You Yourself, the Word-made-flesh may dwell in me. Take away every sinful desire to reject You and have nothing to do with You. Rather, by Your Spirit, through Your Word and Sacraments, come to me and dwell with me that I may never be separated from the Father's love which You have revealed in Yourself. Lord, when You ascended into heaven, You did not shed Your body, but You are true God and man for all eternity. And You still come to me in the flesh, through the Word, the water of Baptism, and the Body and Blood of Your Supper. Let me receive You in these holy ways where You come to me and forgive me. Let me receive You in true faith, confessing not only Your Incarnation but Your coming to me by blood and water in Your holy Church.

Lord Jesus Christ, Your perfect, spotless, sinless flesh is my salvation. By taking it on, You have become my Savior, for then You could suffer and die and rise again. You took upon Yourself my sins and my infirmities. Therefore, be with all those who are weak in the flesh, and who suffer in their lives, especially *(names)*. When their flesh and bodies fail them, let Your perfect and saving flesh be their comfort. When death approaches, let Your eternal flesh that has conquered death, be their hope and strength. By Your coming through Your Word and Sacraments, keep them in the holy faith unto eternal life.

Jesus Christ, Son of God, I call You Lord because You have become man to save me. Teach me that Your being Lord is all about Your work of saving me from my sins. Do not let me fear You as the One who condemns, but rejoice that You are the One whom the Father has sent to save me from my sins and make me His own. All thanks and praise be to You, O Son of God, for Your obedience to Your Father and Your holy incarnation by which You came and conquered all sin and death. I praise You and glorify You, who lives and reigns with the Father and the Holy Spirit, one God, now and forever. Amen.

The Second Article, Part 2

And in Jesus Christ, His only Son, our Lord, who was conceived by the Holy Spirit, born of the Virgin Mary, suffered under Pontius Pilate, was crucified, died and was buried. He descended into hell. The third day He rose again from the dead. He ascended into heaven and sits at the right hand of God, the Father Almighty. From thence He will come to judge the living and the dead.

> *What does this mean? ...who has redeemed me, a lost and condemned person, purchased and won me from all sins, death, and from the power of the devil; not with gold or silver, but with His holy, precious blood and with His innocent suffering and death. This is most certainly true.*

Lord Jesus Christ, Son of God, when I was a slave to sin, You redeemed me. When I was lost, You found me. When I was condemned, You took my place and set me free. When I was sold into death and condemnation, You bought me back with Your suffering and blood. When I was a prize of the evil one, You defeated him and won me back to God. When I was dead in trespasses and sins, Your blood forgave them and gave me life. When I was under the curse of death, You triumphed over death for me. When I was under the power of the devil, You rescued me and brought me into Your kingdom. All praise and thanks be to You, and to You alone, Lord Jesus, for this salvation unearned by me and freely accomplished and given by You!

Lord, my salvation, my forgiveness, my standing before the Father are all Your work. None of that is mine. Forgive me, by that precious blood that You shed, of any and every notion or idea that somehow I can be acceptable to God apart from you. Protect me from the temptation to think that if I am good enough or do enough good or think certain thoughts or live a certain life, that I can then be pleasing to the Father. Rather, teach me that I am acceptable to Him only in and through You and on account of the righteousness You have given me by Your perfect obedience and death for sinners.

Forgive me also, Lord, for putting my faith in something other than Your death for sinners. Teach me, by the Spirit and Your Word, that Your death and resurrection are my life and hope and comfort and joy in all things. Do not let me fall into the dark pit of despair in which I begin trusting in myself or others for forgiveness and life. Do not let me take my eyes from Your cross and passion by which You have taken away my sins. Teach me that my true treasure is not gold and silver and the things of this world but Your blood and suffering and death. Let me hold fast to these gifts in faith so that every attack of the devil, the world, and the sinful flesh may be thrown down.

Let me also, Lord Jesus, learn from Your suffering and death how great are my sinfulness and my sins. So great and complete is the corruption of my nature, so wicked and evil the thoughts of my heart and the words of my mouth and the actions of my life—so sinful is all of it!— that it took Your death, the death of the Son of God to wash it away. Let Your death teach me the greatness of my sins, Lord, but not to cause me despair and fright. Rather, let me learn to abhor and hate my sins and to rejoice that they have been cast on You and that You willingly took them on in order to take them away. Make me to believe that on that cross, Lord, YOU were indeed the One who was cursed for sins. Make me to believe that on that cross YOU became sin for me and for all sinners and that now, in You, I have become the righteousness of God.

When the temptations of this world surround me, Lord, set before my eyes Your cross and passion, Your suffering and death, the holy and blessed wounds that Your risen body still bears. Let me take comfort from what You have done so that I do not fear my sins and that in You, all temptations would be overcome. Teach me to live in Your holy Gifts. Let me live in my Baptism by which Your blood is sprinkled upon me by water and the Word. Let me trust in my pastor's Absolution, where the saving benefits of Your cross are bestowed upon me. Make me to hunger and thirst for righteousness and be satisfied by the eating and drinking of Your Body and Your Blood in the Holy Sacrament. In these ways, bestow upon me and all Your people the holy and saving treasures which are more to be desired than gold and jewels: Your blood and suffering and forgiveness.

Lord Jesus Christ, I bring to You those who are suffering and who need my prayers on their behalf. I ask that You have mercy upon *(names)*. Guard them from the temptations of unbelief and despair that their afflictions bring. For the sake of that same blood that was shed for all people, forgive them whatever sins of worry, anger, frustration, or anything else that may overtake them. By Your Word and Spirit, lift up their heads also to behold You and Your cross and suffering as their hope and joy. Let their suffering be sanctified by Your suffering so that they may be comforted knowing that You, the Son of God, have shared in all their sorrows and troubles. As You bore their sins on the cross, remind them that You have also borne their infirmities, that their hope and trust in You may never fail. And finally, may all of me, at the day of my death, always have before me Christ crucified, my only comfort against all sin, death and the devil and the judgment of the Law. Preserve me, Lord Jesus, in that holy faith which clings only to You and trusts You alone for all of my good and everlasting life. I ask it in Your name, for You live and reign with the Father and the Holy Spirit, one God, now and forever. Amen.

The Second Article, Part 3

And in Jesus Christ, His only Son, our Lord, who was conceived by the Holy Spirit, born of the Virgin Mary, suffered under Pontius Pilate, was crucified, died and was buried. He descended into hell. The third day He rose again from the dead. He ascended into heaven and sits at the right hand of God, the Father Almighty. From thence He will come to judge the living and the dead.

> *What does this mean? ...that I may be His own and live under Him in His kingdom and serve Him in everlasting righteousness, innocence, and blessedness, just as He is risen from the dead, lives and reigns to all eternity. This is most certainly true.*

Lord Jesus Christ, Your disciples despaired when You died upon the cross. Your enemies rejoiced to see Your death. But in Your descent into hell, You proclaimed Your victory over sin and death to Satan and on the third day You stripped death of its power and sting when You rose. The sorrow of Your disciples was turned to joy and not even death itself could ever take away their happiness in You. Now grant me the same joy in Your resurrection from the dead that I would never fall into despair. Give to me that peace with which You breathed upon Your disciples on Easter, the peace of sins forgiven and the knowledge that Your victory over sin and death has become my victory over those enemies.

The Holy Scriptures teach me that You died for me and rose, that I might no longer live for myself but for You, who died for me. Forgive me, Lord, for forgetting this, for ignoring it, for confessing Your resurrection but still living as if sin rules my life. Forgive me for celebrating Easter while still living toward You and others as if death matters. Such thinking causes me to despise Your Word and Gifts, to think them as being of no account. Such thinking causes me to despise others and to treat them as nothing more than hindrances to my own happiness. Lord, by the very same death and resurrection I confess in the Creed, save me from these sins! Save me from a false faith which only makes Your work into some sort of knowledge or just facts and information. Rather, enlighten and enliven me by the Holy Spirit and Your Word and Sacraments to truly believe and trust in Your victory over sin and death. Let me learn to live with such a glad confidence in Your finished work of salvation that every word, thought, and action gives You glory and serves and helps my neighbor.

Lord Jesus Christ, You taught me that this world is passing away. Here I have no enduring city or kingdom. My citizenship is in heaven. Thanks and praise be to You for rescuing me from this kingdom of death and sin that is passing away and for bringing me, by Your death, into Your kingdom. Teach me to confess You as my true and only Lord, and not as a dictator, but as You are: my gracious Lord in whom I have life and salvation. Grant me always to be a faithful and honorable citizen of the earthly lands in which I live. But more than that, let me never forget that I am in Your kingdom, which is the only kingdom that will endure forever. Comfort me against the sorrows of this world passing away by the sure and certain hope which being in Your kingdom gives. Especially do I pray for *(names)* who suffer much. For them and all who are afflicted by the perils and sorrows and misery of this world, I ask Your blessing and comfort, Your strength and peace. Grant to them the strength of Your death and resurrection that they would neither fear sickness, trouble, or even death and that they would be comforted and look forward to their resurrection to eternal life.

Lord, my sins trouble me, the devil seeks to rule my conscience and accuse me, the world and my sinful nature overwhelm me! Give me, by the faithful preaching of Christ crucified and risen, by the remembrance of my Baptism, which makes Your death and resurrection my own, by the Absolution which bestows on me Your saving forgiveness, by Your Body and Blood by which You live in me—by these Gifts give me true comfort and peace against all my enemies. By Your Word and Gifts, show me that, in You, I am truly righteous, innocent, and blessed now and for all eternity. All glory, honor, thanks, and praise be to You, Lord Jesus Christ, for You have become man, taken my sins, died for them, and risen again. Now I am Your own and nothing can snatch me from Your hand. For You live and reign over Your holy and everlasting kingdom with the Father and the Holy Spirit, one God, now and forever. Amen.

The Third Article, Part 1

I believe in the Holy Spirit, the holy Christian church, the communion of saints, the forgiveness of sins, the resurrection of the body, and the life everlasting. Amen.

What does this mean? I believe that I cannot by my own reason or strength believe in Jesus Christ, my Lord, or come to Him; but the Holy Spirit has called me by the Gospel, enlightened me with His gifts, sanctified and kept me in the true faith. This is most certainly true.

O Holy Spirit, Comforter and Giver of life, receive my prayer of thanks for Your work of bringing me into Christ's kingdom. I would never know of Jesus' death and resurrection for sinners except that You have broadcast it to the world through the preaching of the Gospel and the administration of the holy Sacraments. Lord, I was born dead in trespasses and sins. I was brought into this world in darkness. Turned inward, an enemy of God, I was nothing but an object of God's wrath, unable to save myself and unable to turn away from sin and evil. But it was You, Holy Spirit, through the Word and water of my Baptism, who called me, enlightened me, and made me holy in Christ.

Forgive me for every false thought and false faith which trusts in myself to believe in You. Teach me that faith itself, the very act of believing, is Your gift alone, without which I would perish. Let me never trust in my own heart or even in my faith, as if it is by my own reason and willpower that I could become and remain a Christian. Cast far from me every false belief that trusts something in myself and my own will. Guard me from every temptation to believe that I have some measure of good in me by which I can choose my religion and God. Rather, stir up in me always a sanctified heart that gives thanks for the unearned gift of salvation won by my Lord Jesus and given to me in the holy Means of Grace.

Holy Spirit, I thank You for Your saving work in the holy Means of Grace. I thank You for the water and Word of Holy Baptism, in which I was sprinkled with the blood of Jesus, rescued from sin and death, and given God's name upon me. I thank You for Holy Absolution in which my pastor speaks in Christ's place to forgive my sins. I give You thanks for the Word, written by Your inspiration in the Holy Scriptures and preached and taught in the Church. I thank You for the Body and Blood of Jesus, by which He comes to me and forgives me. By these holy Gifts and these alone, You sanctify me, make me holy, and keep me in the true faith of Christ. By these same Gifts, Holy Spirit, preserve me in that faith of Christ until the day of my death, that I may fall asleep in Jesus, comforted by His gifts against all fear of sin and death.

Forgive me, Lord, for turning away from and despising Your Means of Grace. Forgive me for seeking Your Word and will, or presence and blessings apart from the water, the Word, and the Body and Blood. Forgive me for trying to figure You out and know You apart from the ways in which You have promised to come to me and be with me. Guard me, Holy Spirit, from every temptation to look for God working apart from the Means of Grace. Let me not fall under the influence of any preaching or teaching that directs me to my heart or life or circumstances to know my faith. Rather, when I doubt or am afraid or worried, draw me again to the waters of my baptism, the forgiveness declared by my pastor, the Word in the Scriptures and preaching, and the Holy Supper. With these and these alone, grant me comfort against all sin, doubt, and the attacks of the devil, the world, and my sinful nature. Let me never go beyond Your Word and Sacraments to seek You, lest I fall into despair to see God apart from Christ and His mercy.

Lord, I pray that the Word and Sacraments, by which You come to me, would be the strong tower and shield in which I take refuge. Having these Gifts means having Christ and having Him means having all things in heaven and earth. Therefore, let the holy Gifts by which You keep me in the faith also be my comfort against all suffering and death. Let these holy Gifts be a comfort also to *(names)*. Do not let them despair in any trouble but let them cling also to Christ in these Gifts in which He has promised to be present for my life and salvation. Where people suffer who do not know Christ through these Gifts, I pray that You would bring these Gifts to them that they too may be called, gathered, enlightened, sanctified, and kept in the true faith. Let no one perish without the benefit of these holy things, so that they may not perish apart from Christ.

Holy Spirit, You are called the Comforter for good reason, for Your work is to bring me the comfort of Jesus against all sin and death and hell and the wrath of God. For in the Word and Sacraments, You bring Jesus to me, and having Him, I have all I need. Let me always know and believe this as Your true work: to point me to Jesus and to deliver Him to me. Keep me from speaking about You and Your Work as if it is somehow unrelated to the Son and the delivery of His gifts. Make me to know how it is You work among me by giving Christ into me, for He is the One to whom You bear witness. All praise and thanks, O Holy Spirit, that Your work has been fulfilled in me through the preaching of Jesus Christ my Savior. I therefore exalt and magnify You and give You all glory and honor along with the Father and the Son, with whom You are One God, now and forever. Amen.

The Third Article, Part 2

I believe in the Holy Spirit, the holy Christian church, the communion of saints, the forgiveness of sins, the resurrection of the body, and the life everlasting. Amen.

> *What does this mean? In the same way He calls, gathers, enlightens, and sanctifies the whole Christian Church on earth, and keeps it with Jesus Christ in the one true faith. In this Christian Church He daily and richly forgives all my sins and the sins of all believers. This is most certainly true.*

All thanks and praise be to You, Lord Jesus Christ, for You have purchased and won for Yourself a kingdom into which You have brought me by Your Holy Spirit. This is the holy Christian Church. She is my Mother, for by the womb of the font I am given new birth from above. She is the ark in which I escape the judgment and wrath of God against all sins. She is the true Israel, Your chosen people called by grace alone to be the ones among whom You dwell. The Church is Your Bride, washed and made holy and beautiful in Your sight that You may receive Her as Your own on the great day of Your eternal wedding feast. She is the new Eve, brought forth by the water and blood from Your side on the cross, as Eve was brought forth from Adam's rib. She is Your body, You Her Head, and in Her I too am a member of Your holy body. It is Your Church, Lord, where the holy Gospel is preached purely and the holy Sacraments administered rightly that I can be sure You Yourself are present to forgive and save me.

Forgive me for every effort I make to find God apart from Your Church. Remove from me the guilt of my sins which seek God apart from His Word and the Means of Grace. Teach me, by the Holy Spirit and the Word, that where Your Means of Grace are, there and only there can I be certain of Your grace and mercy and my forgiveness and everlasting life. Let this be for my comfort, so that I do not wander in the darkness of this world, looking for You in places You have not promised to be for me.

Forgive me for desiring the Church to be something other than it is, to be for a purpose other than You have given it. Your Church, O Lord, is the place in which You Yourself dwell for the forgiveness of my sins. Forgiveness is why You came into this world, to take away my sins. Forgiveness is why You instituted Holy Baptism, Holy Absolution and Your Holy Supper. Forgiveness of sins is why You commissioned Your Apostles to preach to the ends of the earth. Forgiveness is why You call and ordain men to be pastors, so that I, Your redeemed child, might never doubt Your grace and mercy, but always have Your cross-won forgiveness delivered to me. Teach me always that this forgiveness is what Your Church is about so that I may rejoice to stand before You now and on the Last Day with confidence.

But also, O Lord, I by myself am not Your Church. Your Church is all those whom You have drawn to You by the preaching of the Gospel. As I live, let me not forget my brothers and sisters in Christ around the world but also and especially those in the congregation of which I am a part. I thank You that You have called them also to be members of the body of Christ. Let Your Church be the place in which I learn to love and serve my neighbor to Your glory. When there are those brothers and sisters in Christ who frustrate me—and whom I frustrate!—teach me to live and view others, not as objects of irritation and anger, but as those whom You have redeemed. Teach me to love and forgive others and to do what I can to help and care for them. For my brothers and sisters in Christ in need I pray, especially *(names)*. Keep them in Your loving care and stir me up to whatever good works I can do to help and serve them. I pray also for those who are outside of Your Church, including *(names)*, that by Your grace You would bring to them Your Word, and, that by Your Word, the Holy Spirit would enlighten them and call them into Your Church.

It is by Your grace alone that You have brought me into Your Church for I should otherwise always have remained in the darkness of sin and death. But You have brought me and all believers into Your kingdom and made me Your own. I give You thanks, Lord Jesus, that You have not left me to myself or laid upon me the impossible burden of converting myself. Rather, through the washing of water and the Word, You have poured out Your Spirit upon me so that, being justified by Your grace, I am now heirs of everlasting life. By the same Means of Grace by which You have brought me into the Church, so keep me in Your holy Church, the ark of Your salvation, until at last I come to the blessed new heaven and earth which You will make on the Last Day for me. I, along with all the other members of Your body, Lord Jesus, worship You, my Head, with the Father and the Holy Spirit, one God, now and forever. Amen.

The Third Article, Part 3

I believe in the Holy Spirit, the holy Christian church, the communion of saints, the forgiveness of sins, the resurrection of the body, and the life everlasting. Amen.

What does this mean? On the Last Day He will raise me and all the dead, and give eternal life to me and all believers in Christ. This is most certainly true.

Lord Jesus Christ, I who have been born from above by water and the Spirit, who eat and drink Your flesh and blood, have Your unshakeable promise that You will raise me up on the Last Day. Your holy Apostle Paul writes that I shall be raised imperishable, and your Apostle Peter writes that I have an inheritance kept in heaven that shall never perish, spoil, or fade. Just as the Spirit breathed life into the first man, Adam, and he became a living being; just as the Spirit breathed into the valley of dry bones to awaken the Israelites from death; just as by Your Word young and old woke up from the sleep of death; and above all, as You Yourself came triumphant from the tomb on Easter; so I have Your promise that I too will be raised in my body on the Last Day, awakened from the sleep of death, and given eternal life on the day that You make all things new.

Forgive me, therefore, Lord, for every attempt to cling to this world and this life. The creation of the Father is wonderful and a blessing to me. Yet after sin came it has fallen and become cursed. This is no longer my enduring city; my citizenship is with You. Forgive me for ever thinking there is nothing beyond this life, that I must do what I can now to make myself happy, and that what is most important is my life now. Forgive me for such sins that deny Your promise and the hope of the resurrection of the flesh. On the other hand, let me not become so detached from this world, awaiting the glory to come, that I neglect to live faithfully in my callings and to serve those around me in good works and holy living. Forgive me, Lord, for a fear of death which is greater than the fear that is due You. Forgive me for every sin that seeks to avoid death as if there were nothing on the other side. Remind me again by Your Holy Spirit how You have, by Your triumph over death, turned death into nothing more than sleep for a time until You awaken me on the Last Day. Let me live as You have lived, spurning the shame of the cross and death and looking forward to the glory that is to come.

Guard me also, Lord, from the temptation to dismiss that which is physical, earthly, and of the body. I confess the resurrection of the body! Do not let me live as if escaping from my body is the ultimate goal! Rather, because You Yourself have become man teach me to value and care for my body as Your gift, knowing that it must one day be planted in the ground so that it may be raised imperishable. Guard me also against all false doctrine and teaching concerning the life to come. Protect me from the false teachings that say You will come and establish an earthly kingdom for a time, or that heaven is just clouds and angels, or that I become an angel upon death, or that I am reincarnated or I cease to be an individual and just become part of the cosmos. From all such false teachings preserve me! Fill my ears with the promise that being washed, being forgiven, being full of Your Body and Blood means that my body will rise and my eternal joy will be seeing You face to face in the new heavens and new earth.

Lord, since this world is passing away, I know that I will face much suffering and that the body I have now will not last forever but fall into sickness and death and decay. Open my eyes to that fact so that I do not foolishly pretend I can live forever by my own strength. I pray for those who are sick and suffering, especially *(names)*: let them not despair but take comfort that You will raise them up again and that, in Christ, they will have eternal life. Comfort me also Lord, by Your resurrection, when I mourn the deaths of my loved ones and friends. I remember in particular those who have died, *(names)*. Let me rejoice for those who have died in the faith and now rest from their labors. Remind me that they are a part of that great "cloud of witnesses" by which I am surrounded. Comfort me with the knowledge that they are with You in paradise—with You and the angels and archangels and all the company of heaven. Let me also be comforted with the truth that when the Spirit raises me up on the Last Day, the dead in Christ shall rise, too, and I shall be together in the company of saints who live in the brightness of Your eternal presence forever.

I give You thanks, Lord Jesus, for Your triumph over death by Your resurrection on the third day. Let me so cling to You by faith that I may know the hope of my resurrection from the dead on the Last Day. Keep me in the holy faith until that day I fall asleep in You, and let me rest until You awaken me to glory on the Day You come again—the Day when I shall see Your glory and the Father's and the Holy Spirit's, one God forever. Amen.

The Introduction

Our Father who art in heaven.

What does this mean? With these words God tenderly invites us to believe that He is our true Father and that we are His true children, so that with all boldness and confidence we may ask Him as dear children ask their dear father.

Father in heaven, You have invited me to pray. You have taught me that through my Baptism into Jesus, His Father is now my Father. In the Holy Commandments, You have taught me to call upon You in every trouble, to pray, praise, and give thanks. In the words of the Creed, I have learned that above all things, You are first and foremost, my gracious Father, from whom I have been given all things of body and soul. Now, heavenly Father, hear my prayer as I come before You in the same way that a child would ask something of his dear father.

Forgive me for not approaching You in this way. Forgive me for indifference in my prayers and neglecting to pray at all. You, who have given me all things, tenderly invite me to pray, and I fail to do so. Because of laziness or not trusting that You hear my prayers, or because I don't know the words to use, or not thinking it's important—for these and many other sinful reasons I fail to pray as I should. Prayer does not come naturally. I am not born knowing how to do it. I must, as Jesus' own disciples did, ask Him to teach me to pray. Therefore, Father, put upon my lips always the very words of Jesus for my prayers. In His prayer, He has taught me all good things that You want me to ask from You because You have promised to hear me. Therefore, open my lips that my mouth may declare Your praise. Teach me to take up the cup of salvation and call upon the name of the Lord!

Father, when I pray, let it not be done weakly and in doubt. Rather, teach me to pray with all boldness and confidence! Teach me the pray as Abraham who begged You to spare even 10 righteous people in the city of Sodom. Teach me to pray as Moses who told You to repent of destroying the idolatrous children of Israel. Teach me to pray as David who stood bravely before the enemy Goliath. Teach me to pray as Solomon did who beheld Your glory filling the Temple. Teach me to pray as Your Son prayed, calling upon You with firm trust and confidence. Teach me to pray as St. Paul and the other Apostles, boldly asking You for whatever they and others needed. Remind me that the Holy Spirit also cries out for me with unutterable groans even when I myself don't seem to have the words. Comfort me with the blessed truth that my Lord Jesus Himself stands before Your throne to intercede and pray for me. Then, Father, may I come before You not demanding as if owed, but anchored in Your Word and promises, so that I ask nothing weakly or in doubt, but in boldness and confidence!

When I call upon You, dear Father in heaven, let it be not only for all my own needs but also for my brothers and sisters in Christ and for all people. Here I make known to You my prayers on behalf of others, including *(names)*. As much as You have taught me to trust in You as my dear Father, so grant to each of them the same trusting faith that looks to You for every good and blessing, for all protection and strength, for healing and comfort, for patience and steadfastness. Let all those who have some need, small or great, cry out to You also in boldness and confidence, eagerly awaiting and expecting Your help.

Father, without Your Son taking on flesh and taking away my sins, and without Baptism, the forgiveness of sins, and the Body and Blood of Jesus, I would never be able to call You my Father. Without such grace and mercy and salvation from Jesus, I would never dare to approach Your throne of grace. Indeed, without my Lord's teaching, I would never even know how to pray. Therefore, I give You thanks for revealing Yourself as my dear Father in and through Jesus Christ so that I may learn to call upon You in every need and to believe that You do indeed hear my prayers and answer them according to Your gracious will. Teach me in my prayers to learn more and more what it means that You are my gracious and merciful heavenly Father, who, with Your Son and the Holy Spirit, lives and reigns, one God, forever and ever. Amen.

The First Petition

Hallowed be Thy name.

What does this mean? God's name is certainly holy in itself, but we pray in this petition that it may be kept holy among us also.

How is God's name kept holy? God's name is kept holy when the Word of God is taught in its truth and purity, and we, as the children of God, also lead holy lives according to it. Help us to do this, dear Father in heaven! But anyone who teaches or lives contrary to God's Word profanes the name of God among us. Protect us from this, heavenly Father!

Lord God, heavenly Father, Your Name is indeed holy. It is pure and righteous and perfect. I pray, Father, that the Name of God would be holy to me also. Grant that through Your Word I would know Your Name and to call upon You in every trouble, to pray, praise and give thanks. Forgive me when I have used Your Name like a common curse word. Even more, forgive me for not clinging to Your Name to call upon You for all things that I need. Forgive me for my unbelief and despising of Your Name. You have given me Your Name as gift to use and I have not prayed and called upon it as I should. For the sake of Jesus, whose very Name means "the Lord saves," save me from my sins! Hear me as I call upon Your Name so that, with Your Name put upon upon me in Holy Baptism, I may trust that You are my Father and that You know me as Your child.

(FOR PASTORS)

Lord, Your Name is holy when Your Word is taught in its truth and purity. You have called me to the holy Office through which Your Word is preached in the world and to Your people in particular. Therefore, grant to me faithfulness in preaching and teaching Your holy Word. Forgive me for every sin which seeks to avoid studying and learning Your Word so that I may teach it rightly. Forgive me for putting other things above Your Word and seeking other treasure than that which You give in Your Word. Stir up my heart to love Your Word, to desire it more than gold, even fine gold, and even more than honey from the comb. As I study the Holy Scriptures, read them, learn them, and preach and teach them, let my mind be focused upon the task so that my thoughts do not wander. Teach me to see Christ throughout the Holy Scriptures so that I might faithfully preach Him crucified. Grant me Your Holy Spirit so that I may rightly divide the Word of truth, preaching the Law so that sinners are driven to seek refuge in Christ and preaching the Gospel so that sinners are comforted against all sin and death. Teach me to apply Your Word in whatever measure is needed by those who hear it so that they may be rebuked or exhorted or encouraged or comforted as they should.

Guard me, Lord, from every temptation to silence Your Word with my own opinions or thoughts. Protect me from every peril and trap of the devil which would turn my preaching and teaching into false doctrine and lies. Guard me from preaching and teaching in such a way that those who are secure in their sins are not driven from them in fear and that those who weep for comfort despair of Your mercy! Above all, let me never preach and teach in such a way that people take any confidence and delight in me, but only in Christ and Your gifts and promises. Forgive me and guard me still from every desire to make doctrine something unimportant or to think that there could be anything more pressing than rightly understanding Your holy Word. Also keep me, Father, from every thought, word, and deed that would contradict the faithful preaching of Your Word. Do not let me fall into any sins that would be contrary to Your Word. In thoughts, words, and deeds, let my life match my preaching so that Your Name is never profaned and made common.

(FOR HEARERS)

Your Word, Lord, is to be taught in its truth and purity. Jesus said that He Himself is the Truth and that the Holy Spirit would lead me into all truth. Therefore, grant that I and all Your people may know the truth of Christ through the right preaching of Your Word, so that Your Name may be holy among me. To that end, I pray for my pastor. Grant him the patience and wisdom to learn Your Word and so be a faithful teacher of it.

Grant that my pastor would never preach or teach anything other than Christ and Him crucified for the forgiveness of my sins. I know, Lord, that any pastor has many responsibilities, many people to care for, and many duties to carry out. But let nothing hinder him from being able to preach faithfully what Your people need to hear. Guard my pastor from all sickness and harm that would remove his voice from Your flock. Protect him from petty distractions and material worries which would draw his heart and mind away from his shepherding task. Let none of Your people ever become a hindrance to his ministry but rather let me submit myself to his pastoral care so that his work may be a joy and not a burden! Forgive me whenever I have neglected to pray for my pastor. Most especially guard him from such temptations of the flesh that would cause him to forsake or be removed from this holy Office. If it should be that my pastor falls into some sin or turns from the right preaching of Your Word, help me to restore him gently, urge upon him true repentance, and be blessed by his faithful ministry once again.

Teach me also, as Your child, to faithfully hear, read, and understand Your Word, that Your Name may be holy to me. Since You have given me a faithful preacher, do not let my heart and mind wander to other churches, other preachers, other ways of hearing Your so-called Word. Teach me to beware of those who would draw me away from Christ and His Word by seductive preaching that flatters me and makes me feel good while delivering nothing of Jesus and the forgiveness of sins. Let me never be attracted by false doctrines, horoscopes, prophecies, "end-times" preaching, slick and clever sounding preachers, or anything else that is not Your Word true and pure, but rather the lies of the devil. Teach me to rightly discern what is true and pure from what is false and a lie. Teach me by Your faithful pastors to know and understand the Scriptures so that I too may judge all doctrine and be comforted against all sin and death.

+   +   +

Father, You have given me Your holy Word-made-flesh in Jesus Christ to rescue me from sin and death. Your holy written Word also teaches me how, as Your child, I should live so that I might glorify You and love and serve my neighbor. Forgive me for every sin that makes the Name of Christ I bear worthless in the eyes of the world. Though the world will still hate Christ, let His Name that I bear shine as a light in my good works, so that men may see those works and glorify You. Teach me to consider carefully all that I do so that my words and actions will confess Christ and His grace and His working through me for the benefit of others. Let me not be an example for the world of what a Christian is not, and who Christ is not—rather let all I say confess His Name truly and purely and all that I do be in accord with Your Word. Do not let me fear the consequences of living according to Your Word in this world but let me always and joyfully do all things in accordance with Your Word. Grant, Father, to those for whom I pray, especially *(names)*, Your Word of comfort purely taught and a life which is lived in the hope of that Word so that even among those who suffer or have troubles, Your Name is kept holy.

Your Name is holy, Lord. Now, I have prayed that You keep it holy among me. Preserve me until I go again to hear Your Word faithfully preached, be reminded of my Baptism when Your holy Name was put upon me, be absolved in Your Name, hear the Name of Christ preached, and hear Him speaking to give me His Body and Blood. Grant that the preaching and teaching I hear in church would fill my ears and heart and mind so that as I go back out into the world, I may live as a Christian, that is, "little Christ", being a shining light to the world in the ways that Your Word teaches me to do. Because the Name of Jesus is a holy, saving Name, I ask all these things in and through His Name. Amen.

The Second Petition

Thy kingdom come.

What does this mean? The kingdom of God certainly comes by itself without our prayer, but we pray in this petition that it may come to us also.

How does God's kingdom come? God's kingdom comes when our heavenly Father gives us His Holy Spirit, so that by His grace we believe His holy Word and lead godly lives here in time and there in eternity.

Lord God, heavenly Father, by the Holy Spirit, You have breathed life into me through Your Word. If You should take Your Holy Spirit from me, I would perish, covered by the darkness of my sins and without hope. Therefore, always give me Your Holy Spirit that I may believe Your Word and not only that but live in this life as Your dear child according to Your Word. I am born into this world into the kingdom of the evil one, under his power and a slave to his evil. But You have rescued me by the sending of Your Son Jesus Christ to destroy the devil's power and make me Your own. Grant that I who have been brought into this kingdom may never forsake it nor be taken from it. Your own Son has promised that I shall never be snatched from Your hands. You have established Your kingdom in this world through Your Word and it remains to this day even though earthly kingdoms and nations rise and fall. Keep me in Your kingdom by Your Holy Spirit that I may rejoice to live in this kingdom forever and ever.

Forgive me for ever thinking that I do not need Your Spirit to believe. Forgive me for thinking that apart from Your Word and Spirit I can do anything that pleases you. By my own efforts and because of my own accomplishments I desire You to smile upon me. Yet apart from Christ, all my righteous deeds are as filthy rags. Teach me that in Christ my life is holy on His account and never my own. Let me never trust in myself and my own strength but in You who are my Rock and Fortress. Remind me also that I have no holy life apart from Your Spirit dwelling in me. Do not let me take pride in my good works as if they are not done by Christ living in me. Guard me from every temptation to make my Christian life a matter of how well I am improving or what things I am doing.

Grant me true and saving faith which clings to Your Word and promises. By the Holy Spirit confirm in me the gifts given in Holy Baptism, the letting loose of all my sins by the Holy Absolution, and the truth that Christ lives in me through His Body and Blood given in His Supper. Protect me against all doubt and despair and worry and unbelief by the never-failing gifts of Your Word and Sacraments. By these and these alone, let me be certain that I have Christ and having Him, be certain my sins are forgiven and my life is holy before You.

Forgive me also, Lord, when I take what I confess of Your Word and salvation and make it into nothing more than facts and knowledge. Blot out every sin in which I confess You with my lips but deny You with my life and actions. Stir me up to holy living and good works which are Your glory and the blessing and service of those around me. Let me not be a hearer only but also a doer of Your Word. Because it is no longer I who live, but Christ who lives in me, then through Him accomplish in my life whatever will benefit others and be a faithful and living witness to Christ. In every thought, word, and action, let me decrease and my neighbor increase. Remove from me all selfishness and the desire to only serve and please myself. Grow in me that holy fruit of the Spirit by which I am a blessing to others and a help and comfort to them.

Lord, for those who suffer, those who are in trouble, and especially those who suffer doubts or despair—here I pray for *(names)*—do not take Your Spirit from them, lest they be overwhelmed and taken from Your kingdom. Rather, by Your Word and Gifts, pour out Your Spirit upon them so that they would be kept firm in the holy faith of Christ. Let Your Spirit be especially upon all those who are in danger of falling away and denying the true faith, especially *(names)*. Drive away from them the evil one, the worthless lies of the world and their sinful flesh, so that they may be preserved as Your child in this life. Do not let those whom You have so graciously brought into Your kingdom fall again from it and perish forever. Rather, hold them in Your hand and direct them again to the comforting voice of the Good Shepherd who knows them.

Finally, heavenly Father, I pray for Your kingdom to come wherever it has not yet. To nations and tribes and peoples and individuals that have not heard the Gospel of the forgiveness of sins for Christ's sake, send Your preachers. Be with all pastors and with all missionaries as they bring the light of Your Word so that the Holy Spirit might establish Your kingdom wherever Christ is preached. Then, O Lord, when I stand before You on the Last Day, gathered from all peoples, tribes, languages—a host without number—I shall sing Your praises for all eternity in Your kingdom which has no end. I pray in the name of Jesus Christ, whose kingdom comes to me, who is the King of Kings and Lord of Lords. Amen.

The Third Petition

Thy will be done on earth as it is in heaven.

What does this mean? The good and gracious will of God is done even without our prayer, but we pray in this petition that it may be done among us also.

How is God's will done? God's will is done when He breaks and hinders every evil plan and purpose of the devil, the world, and our sinful nature, which do not want us to hallow God's name or let His kingdom come; and when He strengthens and keeps us firm in His Word and faith until we die.

This is His good and gracious will.

Heavenly Father, it was Your will that Your Son should rescue me from sin and death. Where I was disobedient, He was faithful and obedient to You in all things, thus winning my salvation. It is Your will that the Gospel of the forgiveness of sins be preached in Jesus' name to the ends of the earth. It is Your will that, by Your Word, by Water, and by Christ's Body and Blood, I be brought into the holy faith of Your Church and be kept in that faith until my dying day. It is Your will that I do not perish but have everlasting life through Jesus Christ. Therefore, Father, let not the will of the devil nor that of the world nor the desires of my sinful flesh overcome Your will. Preserve and keep me in this holy faith and guard and defend me against all of these enemies!

Father, the devil is that ancient serpent, that deceiver and the father of lies. He has been a liar from the beginning, and he desires that if he cannot have Your power and glory, then he will rob me of my joy and happiness in You. From the first moments of the Garden of Eden, the devil has twisted Your Word and lied about Your promises in order to deceive me. He succeeded, and mankind fell into sin! Now, through all false religions and false preaching, he still seeks to turn my heart and mind from Christ. With lies he tempts me to believe that I can save myself or that there is no God. With his false religions on the one hand, he seeks to deceive me into trusting in false and nonexistent gods. On the other hand, he tries to trick me with the teachings of the world that claim there is no God and nothing spiritual with which to concern myself. He is Satan, the Accuser, who tries to burden my conscience with the knowledge of my sins and the lie that my sins shall cause me to perish. Break and hinder every one of his evil plans and purposes! Guard me from his lies and, by the true and faithful preaching of Your Word, let Your will be done, that I would be kept in the true faith and believe alone in Christ my Lord, knowing without doubt that my sins are truly forgiven, that I am Your child, and that the evil one has no power over me who is in Christ Jesus!

Also, Father, there is the world. The world has gone its own way from the very first. From Cain, who left his father and mother to make his own way in the world, to the wicked generation of Noah, which You destroyed by the Flood, to the nations and kingdoms that continue to rise and fall and that deny that You are the true King of all peoples, the world has turned from You and seeks to exalt itself. Through false knowledge and a religious devotion to "science" and "reason," the world seeks to live as if what is unseen cannot possibly exist. The world denies the very evidence of its Maker, and it shuts its ears to the preaching of the Savior. Having escaped, as it supposes, the shackles of religion, the world teaches that anything is possible, anything is allowable. Every lifestyle and way of living, of serving myself, of getting the most while I can in this life, regardless of what misery I cause others—all these ways of greed and self-promotion are taught in the world so that I learn to love nothing but myself. This world, which has rejected You, Father, is perishing. Protect me from this fate by turning me in true repentance to faith in Jesus Christ. Break and hinder every plan and purpose of this sinful world which seeks to turn me from faith in Christ to love and trust in myself instead along with all the other things of this world that are passing away. Rescue me, Lord, from the evil with which I am surrounded. Let it never tear me away from Christ but let me have my refuge in Him until the day this world finally passes away and I live in the new heaven and earth, the home of righteousness.

And as if these enemies were not enough, heavenly Father, You know also that my own flesh, my sinful nature is enslaved to the evil one's lies and would gladly go after the wicked things of this world. At every turn, contrary to every Commandment, my sinful nature seeks its own glory and pleasure. My sinful nature means that I do not love You above all things. In fact, I was born as Your enemy, under the curse because of my sinful nature. I certainly do not love my neighbor as myself, but I always put myself above others at every opportunity. But now I have been washed, sanctified, and justified in Your sight through the water, Word, and Spirit of Holy Baptism. In that saving flood, You have drowned that Old Adam, that sinful flesh, and brought forth a New Man clothed in the robe of Christ's perfect righteousness. Therefore, again I beg Your mercy and forgiveness in Jesus so that You will not count against me any of the sins of my flesh. Make me to know by Baptism and Absolution that my sins are forgiven. Give into my mouth the holy flesh and blood of Christ so that with His perfect flesh dwelling in me, I may be raised up on the Last Day, shedding my sinful nature and living in the resurrection body of perfection that is Your gift.

Heavenly Father, these three enemies, the devil, the world, and my sinful nature, plague me to no end. Were it not for Your grace given through Word and Sacrament, I should never remain Your child nor die in the faith of Christ. So again, preserve me against these tyrants who seek my destruction! Father, I ask this same accomplishing of Your will for *(names)* and all those who are in trouble or in any danger or need. Protect them from these enemies that they would never fall away in trouble into despair and unbelief. Keep them also in Your holy Church, in the holy faith of Christ. Lord, so easily does the devil come and snatch away Your Word, the temptations of this world wither its growth, and the cares and pleasures of this life choke it off. Stir up my heart that it may be a fruitful soil in Christ. Fill it with Your Word so that it may by Your grace take root and grow and produce much fruit over and against all my enemies. Let Your Word accomplish Your will in me that I may be kept in that Word and faith until I die. Christ my Lord, by His death and resurrection has been victorious over all these enemies; now His victory is mine! Let it always be so, for such is Your good and gracious will, heavenly Father, as is that of the Son and Holy Spirit, one God, now and forever. Amen.

The Fourth Petition

Give us this day our daily bread.

> *What does this mean? God certainly gives daily bread to everyone without our prayers, even to all evil people, but we pray in this petition that God would lead us to realize this and to receive our daily bread with thanksgiving.*

> *What is meant by daily bread? Daily bread includes everything that has to do with the support and needs of the body, such as food, drink, clothing, shoes, house, home, land, animals, money, goods, a devout husband or wife, devout children, devout workers, devout and faithful rulers, good government, good weather, peace, health, self-control, good reputation, good friends, faithful neighbors, and the like.*

Heavenly Father, You are the giver of every good and perfect gift which comes down from above. Even to those who are not Your children in Christ You give generously all that they need for their bodies and lives. Teach me, Father, always to behold the blessings that You shower upon me and to give thanks for them. You give to me what I need not because I have deserved it but because I am Your dear child in Christ Jesus. Therefore, teach me to realize that all I have comes from You. Help me to receive all that You give me with true and genuine thanksgiving, acknowledging You as the giver of every gift and blessing.

It is not just that You give to me my food or clothing. You provide for a society and government and men and women in various vocations and callings who produce and deliver these goods for my benefit. From the weather that makes growing food possible and in abundance, to those who manufacture and distribute my goods, to those who provide the services that deliver and supply my food and clothing, to the government which protects and defends me from enemies and criminals who would take my goods away, to my parents and employers who provide for me the income to supply my needs—for all of these people, seen and unseen, known and unknown, I give You thanks. Guard, preserve, and protect all people in their godly callings so that my nation may flourish and that You would continue, through these means, to provide for me all that I need each day.

(FOR THE UNEMPLOYED)

Father, it has pleased You to lay upon me the cross of unemployment. If it be Your will, graciously place me into another job in which I may be provided my daily bread and by which I may support and care for my family and those for whom I am responsible. While I am not employed let me not be idle but grant me the strength and motivation to seek work and receive gratefully whatever opportunities with which I am presented. At the same time, let me use this time as a gift to care for my family and others in ways I might not otherwise be able to do. By Your gracious hand, do not forsake me in my time of need, but while I am not working, provide me with whatever I and my family need to survive each day. In Your mercy, spare me from loss of home or lack of food and nutrition. Rather, grant me whatever I need to sustain me. Above all, let my trust in You never fail and through a difficult time such as this, do not let me fall into unbelief and despair. Keep me thankful for all that You give, however large or small, and hold me and mine in Your gracious keeping.

+   +   +

I pray for all families, heavenly Father. Bless all husbands and wives and parents and children that together they would live devout and godly lives. Be with all fathers so that they may provide well for their families and, most of all, teach them to lead their families in the true worship that receives Your gifts of Word and Sacrament. Bless all wives to be a support to their husbands and children both inside and outside the home as they have opportunity. Bless all parents that they may faithfully provide for their children, holding nothing back in selfishness, but generously providing for all that their children need. Bless my children that they may honor and respect the parents You have given them and to recognize them as standing in Your place to provide and care for them. Keep all families in peace, and wherever there is discord and strife, stir up their hearts to repentance and faith, that they would overflow with forgiveness for one another.

I ask Your blessings upon me through my government and those who protect me. Bless the President of my nation, my Congress, my judges, my governors, state representatives, mayors, and city councils with wisdom to lead not in selfishness but for the common good of the people they were elected to serve. Grant safety and courage to all those in my Armed Forces who travel the world to keep me at home in peace and safety. Be with all policemen, firemen, corrections officers, doctors, nurses, paramedics, highway workers, social service workers, and all those in public vocations of service so that they might protect and preserve me against harm and danger and be themselves kept safe in doing so. Grant them integrity and honesty in carrying out these holy callings for the sake of others. Grant that they too may be found in Christ so that they have the highest hope and comfort as they live in these callings.

So that I might enjoy the fruits of the earth and be sustained by them, grant me such good weather as will provide these gifts. Father, in Your mercy, guard me from all storms, lightning, hail, drought, fires, earthquakes, and whatever other disasters by which I would be deprived of my life or those things I need to live. Where such disasters occur—and they will because of this fallen creation—grant that I may continue to receive all that I need to live and make me generous with the gifts I myself have been given to help those whose earthly goods have been lost.

There are so many things I need, heavenly Father, which You graciously provide. Yet in Your Fatherly goodness You provide me with even more than I need, an overflowing abundance of gifts for which I give You thanks. For my friends and neighbors, for my recreation and vacation, for my hobbies and sports, for my gatherings with friends, my holidays and my pastimes, for fine food and drink, for entertainment and some days with no obligations and commitments—for all these gifts above and beyond what I need to live, I give You thanks! Grant me Your Holy Spirit that I may learn to enjoy these things always as a gift from Your Fatherly hand and never to excess or in a way that abuses them and harms others. Forgive me for letting these things become central to my life in such a way that I lose sight of my duty to serve others and glorify You.

As I have been given to graciously and generously, so grant me the heart to give and help others generously with what I myself have been given. Grant me, Lord, never to have so much that I forget You and neither too little that I fall into worry and despair or make sinful attempts to get what I need. Father, for all those who have any trouble or need, especially *(names)*, grant to them a rich supply of whatever it is they may need: food, clothing, shelter, medical care, counseling, job, or friends and loved ones. Let me who has been richly blessed with so much be quick to open my hands in generous giving for their sakes that I too might be the means by which You care for those in need.

Above all, heavenly Father, grant me the True Bread which lasts eternally, that is, the flesh of Jesus Christ given for the life of the world. Above all these earthly gifts You supply, teach me to hunger and thirst for Your Son's flesh Body and Blood that I may be comforted against this world which is passing away. Teach me never to worry over the things of this life as the nations do but to believe that as You, my heavenly Father, always know best what I need and will provide it in due time. Stir up my heart to seek first the Kingdom of God and the righteousness of Christ, knowing Your promise that all these other things will be added unto me. The earthly bread that I am given will sustain me for a while, but eventually death shall come. Therefore, keep me fed with the Bread of Life, even Jesus Christ my Lord, so that when this world passes away, I may enjoy the eternal feast You have prepared for me. I offer these petitions before You on account of the Bread of Life, Jesus Christ, and in and through His holy Name. Amen.

The Fifth Petition

And forgive us our trespasses as we forgive those who trespass against us.

What does this mean? We pray in this petition that our Father in heaven would not look at our sins, or deny our prayer because of them. We are neither worthy of the things for which we pray, nor have we deserved them, but we ask that He would give them all to us by grace, for we daily sin much and surely deserve nothing but punishment. So we too will sincerely forgive and gladly do good to those who sin against us.

Gracious heavenly Father, who in Your mercy sent to me Your only-begotten Son, that He would be my sacrifice for sins and the Savior of all people: I ask today Your forgiveness for all my sins. I know that because of the Fall I am conceived and born in sin. From my mother's womb I am condemned in Your sight because of the iniquity which clings to me, passed down from Adam, through whom sin came into the world. Not only am I corrupted through and through, but my sinful nature leads me into all kinds of actual sins: what I think and say and do. There is no year nor month nor day nor hour in which I am not a sinner. On account of that, I should never dare to ask You for anything. I should expect nothing from You but judgment and punishment: misery in this life and eternal death and condemnation in hell. Therefore, I do not come before You on the basis of my life or good works for I have no standing of myself. Rather I come before You in the Name of Jesus Christ whose blood was shed to take away my sins; whose cross and passion have satisfied Your wrath and taken my punishment; whose resurrection means that the power of sin and death are destroyed. For His sake, hear my prayer. Because I am Your child in Christ, hear my prayer. Because in Him You have forgotten my sins, treat me according to my standing as Your dear child and never according to what my sinfulness deserves.

Send me Your Holy Spirit so that by Your Word I may learn to acknowledge and confess my sins. Let me never hide what I have done but freely confess that I am sinful. Teach me that I do not love You with my whole heart and that I do not love my neighbor as myself. Let me fear Your wrath and not do anything against Your holy Commandments! Yet where I fail and fall short of Your glory, forgive me, for Jesus' sake. For the sake of His suffering, death and resurrection, no longer count my sins against me! Every day and especially in the company of Your Church, answer this prayer for forgiveness with the reminder of my Baptism into Christ in which I am forgiven of my sins, rescued from death and the devil, and given eternal salvation. Answer this prayer for forgiveness with Your words of Holy Absolution, in which the pastor speaks to me and thus Christ Himself is dealing with me, telling me my sins are no more. Answer this prayer for forgiveness by, once again, feeding me with Jesus' Body and Blood so that I may have forgiveness, life, and salvation. Answer this prayer by the faithful preaching and teaching of Christ as my Savior from all sin and death! Let me know that by these holy gifts my sins, no matter how great or small, are truly and completely and eternally forgiven. Therefore, let the evil one never plague and accuse me, but let my confidence be in the full and free forgiveness that is mine in Jesus Christ.

Then, Father, having rejoiced in such a forgiveness for me, teach me to forgive others in the same way. That is, let me cover and overlook their sins as You cover me in Jesus Christ. When someone sins against me, whether in their words or actions, teach me to forgive them. Let me learn that forgiveness means not treating them as their sins may deserve, just as You have not given me what I deserved. Guard me from every temptation to strike back against someone with my own bitter words or to bury my hurt within and carry a bitter and unending grudge against others. Where the pain of another person's sin against me is great, heal me so that I may not bear that pain as a reminder of their sin but gladly forgive and forget what they have done against me. When I have the opportunity to treat someone in accordance with his wrongs, teach me the patience and wisdom and forgiveness to instead deal with him as one for whom Christ died. Even as the servant was forgiven ten thousand talents so let me never wring my neighbor's neck for a few dollars! As I have been forgiven, so let me forgive, lest I be in danger of forfeiting my forgiveness because I will not repent of holding on to my neighbor's sins. Where I am the offender, teach me such humility as to admit my wrong and to ask the forgiveness of those I have hurt and sinned against. Therefore, with Your whole Church that lives from Christ's forgiveness, grant me peace with others.

Lord, let no bitterness prevail in my life but rather joy and peace in the forgiveness of Christ. Where there are some who have hurt me, teach me to forgive them. Especially, grant me to forgive *(names)* and also to be at peace with those whom I have hurt, especially *(names)*. In the midst of suffering and struggles, let none of Your dear children think their sufferings are on account of their sins! Grant to all, especially *(names)* the peace of knowing that whatever crosses they bear, their sins are truly forgiven. Thus guard them from despair and keep them in the faith of Christ, stirring up their hearts to forgive others who may have hurt them. While I should never dare on my own to approach You in prayer, yet in Christ I come boldly and confidently before You as Your dear child. As a father teaches his little ones to get along, so having forgiven me, teach me to live in peace and genuine Christian love for others. This prayer I ask in and through Jesus Christ who has borne my iniquity and washed away all my sins. Amen.

The Sixth Petition

And lead us not into temptation.

What does this mean? God tempts no one. We pray in this petition that God would guard and keep us so that the devil, the world, and our sinful nature may not deceive us or mislead us into false belief, despair, and other great shame and vice. Although we are attacked by these things, we pray that we may finally overcome them and win the victory.

Heavenly Father, it is true that You tempt no one. Yet by the Spirit my Lord was cast into the wilderness to be tempted by the evil one. At every twisting of Your Word, at every temptation to earthly glory, Your Son turned back the devil with the Word of God. He, who is the Word-made-flesh, stood strong against the lies and temptations of the devil thus securing for me my victory over the evil one. When tempted to turn aside from going to the cross for sinners, Your Son did not do His will but Yours and carried out Your command to take the place of sinners and die for them. Even while enduring the tortures of a horrible death, Your Son did not deny You but cried out to You and before He breathed His last, commended His Spirit into Your hands. Jesus' resurrection on Easter shows that by His death He has truly overcome the power of the devil and death. My Baptism into His Name means that His victory has become my victory!

Therefore, because Christ has overcome all these enemies, the devil, the world, and even my own sinful nature and its sins, guard and keep me from every temptation of these enemies that I would never fall away from You but unto my dying day be preserved in Christ unto eternal life. Guard me, Father, from every temptation of the devil. Most especially close my ears to his lies and twisting of Your Word. Turn me away from every false religion and teaching that exalts men and not Christ, that tells me I have the power to save myself, or that claims my good works can make up for my sins. Shut my ears to every false religion and god that would teach me to trust in myself. Protect me also from every lying accusation that says I am not Your child because of my sins. In all these ways the devil would try to deceive me and mislead me into false belief, to trust in something other than Jesus. The devil would have me despair and be uncertain of Your free and full forgiveness in Christ. Therefore, keep me safe in Christ from these temptations.

The world also surrounds me with its temptations. The world, loving itself, puts before me every conceivable enticement to break Your commandments and to live for myself, denying You and caring nothing for my neighbor. Since I am in Christ, secure in my Baptism, filled with Christ's Body and Blood, deliver me, dear Father, by these very things, from every temptation the world sets before me! Deliver me from the desires to ignore Your Word, to stop coming to church, and to spend the time I would use to hear Your Word in doing things that are not so important. Deliver me from every temptation to disrespect my parents or to hurt or harm my children. Guard me from the world's way of quick revenge and murdering with words. Protect me from the filth the world revels in that rejects holy marriage and makes a mockery of the love between husband and wife. Also lead me away from the world's view that any lifestyle and action is acceptable as long as no one is hurt. Block for me every temptation of the world to take what does not belong to me, as if I have a right to something that is not ours. Guard my lips that I may speak no evil of anyone as the world encourages me to do constantly. Finally, Father, grant me holy and peaceful contentment with all that You give me so that I am guarded from the world's lusting and coveting of every kind of mammon and earthly goods. Protect me, heavenly Father from every temptation that would lead me into great shame and vice, dishonoring Your name and harming others.

Were the devil and the world my only enemies, I should be pressed hard on every side and overwhelmed, but my sinful nature, my flesh, also gladly joins in with these to cause my downfall and sin. The temptations of the devil and world are gladly received by my flesh, which cares nothing for God and nothing for neighbor. Therefore, having been baptized into Christ, always give me the Holy Spirit who may live in me and do battle in me with my Old Adam. Every day, let the New Man, raised by the Spirit, come forth to live in righteousness and purity and drown the Old Adam so that he would not rule my life. For the sake of the blood of Jesus shed from

His holy and perfect flesh, turn away Your wrath against me for every temptation to which I have given in. Cleanse me from impure and hateful thoughts, from words that tear others down and deny You, and from actions and deeds that serve only myself and display the filthy idolatry and lusts and coveting of my sinful nature. By Your holy Word and Sacraments, always give me Your Spirit so that I may instead be filled with His fruit, that He may work in me love, joy, peace, patience, kindness, goodness, gentleness and self-control. Crucify in me my fleshly desires and strengthen me to walk in the light of Christ's love. Teach me to rejoice in Your good gifts and to walk gladly in the way of righteousness.

Heavenly Father, these same enemies that plague me also turn the sufferings of Your people into temptations to deny Your goodness and fall away from you. Therefore, by Your Word, send the Holy Spirit to comfort all those who are sick and suffering and protect them from these enemies who would drag them into unbelief and despair. Here I bring before You those who are in trouble and need: *(names)*. Behold them in Your mercy so that whatever things they must suffer that these would not be occasions for them to fall away but rather to strengthen them in Christ and comfort them with Your promises of forgiveness of sins and eternal life.

Finally, I know that in this life these enemies shall never leave me. They shall always come after me to destroy me if they could. Therefore, I pray in Christ's Name and for His sake that You would never abandon me to them. Rescue me from their temptations. Deliver me from their wickedness. As the Israelites who sinned looked up to the bronze serpent and had their lives spared, so turn my eyes of faith to behold Christ, raised up on the cross to deliver me from all these enemies. By Your Word, Baptism, Absolution and the Holy Supper, defend me from all temptations. Hidden in the wounds of Christ, let me ever be safe from all attacks of the evil one, this world, and my own flesh. Deliver and preserve me so that on the Last Day I may celebrate my victory over all these enemies, the victory which is only mine in and through Jesus Christ my Lord, who lives and reigns with You and the Holy Spirit, one God, now and forever. Amen.

The Seventh Petition

But deliver us from evil.

> *What does this mean? We pray in this petition, in summary, that our Father in heaven would rescue us from every evil of body and soul, possessions and reputation, and finally, when our last hour comes, give us a blessed end, and graciously take us from this valley of sorrow to Himself in heaven.*

Dear Father in heaven, at the hour of His death, Your Son commended His Spirit into Your hands. Teach me to live each day doing the same, commending myself to Your care and grace in Jesus Christ. Teach me every night to fall asleep in peace, free from worry, doubt, fear, or any other disturbance of my conscience and faith. Guard me from every evil thing that would frighten me or terrify me or turn me away from Jesus. As Your Son has promised that nothing can snatch me from Your hand, therefore keep such a hold on me in Christ unto my dying day that I may never fear being cut off from You and destroyed.

Rescue me now and my whole life long from every evil of the body. Protect me from illness and sickness, from accident and injury, from suffering of mind and body. I know that these things will come, Father, but I ask that You will prevent them from driving me to despair and dragging me away from faith and trust in You. Rescue me also from every evil of the soul. Protect me from every false teaching and every evil argument given to persuade me to turn away from You and Your Word. Deliver me from everything that would cause me to despair of Your grace in Christ, to lose faith in Him, and to perish eternally apart from Jesus! Be my protection against every evil of my possessions. Deliver me from tragedy and disaster and anything else that would rob me of the means by which I live, my daily bread, my clothing and food and shelter. Should You permit such things to come upon me, then preserve me in the faith and provide me whatever I need for this body and life. Deliver me also, Father, from every evil of reputation. Give to me, as Your child in Christ, honor and a good name among all people, believers and unbelievers alike so that I may give no offense and cause no one to stumble. Guard me from all wickedness that would ruin my reputation such that I become a stumbling block to others. Rather, preserve me in Christ and—no matter what anyone might say or do against me—let their words and actions not cause me to fall away but let my refuge and strength be in Jesus.

Father, in and through Jesus Christ, I know that all the power of the Enemy has been overcome. Even though I will be assaulted by these evils of body and soul and property and honor, I am Your child because of Christ's death for me. His sacrifice for sinners and His resurrection from the dead are my certain hope against all these things. This is why I pray, Father, that You may not let any of these things that come against me prevent me from trusting in Christ or prevent me from receiving my eternal inheritance. Against every evil that I face, lay up the truth of my Baptism into Your name. Place the sure words of Holy Absolution against every hindrance and attack of my enemies. Put the preaching of Christ crucified for me as the frontline defense against every assault of the devil, world, and flesh. Give me Christ Himself, in His Body and Blood, that He may live in me and raise me up on the Last Day, triumphant over every enemy and evil, safe in Him, who is my Savior. Forgive me for every sin of doubt and unbelief that believes these evils can destroy me. Teach me that in Jesus Christ, nothing that is evil can truly harm me and that He Himself is my deliverance from every evil. Let this always be my confidence.

While I suffer these things, and You shelter me in Christ, preserve me also as I walk through the Valley of the Shadow of Death. Father, teach me to die. Teach me that to be in Christ means I will fall asleep in Jesus in peace. Teach me to number my days aright and to be prepared every moment to fall asleep in Christ. Teach me never to fear death. Rather teach me to despise it, mocking its power and fearing it no more than lying in my bed sleeping. When the hour of my death draws near, grant that I would not cower in terror but rejoice in the promise that death, which is now nothing but sleep, is the way in which I am brought to be with You in paradise. At the last hour of my life, let me not fear but cling to Christ in all of His gifts so that I may fall asleep with a glad and happy confidence and await with joy the coming of Christ to raise me on the Last Day. Protect me from violent and sudden death, Father! At every moment let me know that not even death itself can separate me from Your love which is in Christ Jesus. Grant this same protection from all evil and lack of fear of death to everyone whose suffering is great, even those who may be near death, especially *(names)*. Rescue them from whatever evils would cause them doubt and despair and prepare them also to fall asleep in Christ, happy and confident in Your mercy. Deliver me and Your whole Church from the evils that attack us so that together we may sing Your praises here on earth and one day with the whole heavenly host and Your Church triumphant. I long for that day in Christ, dear Father. Keep me in Him until I see that Day. For the sake of Your Son and in His holy Name I pray. Amen.

The Conclusion

[For Thine is the kingdom and the power and the glory forever and ever.] Amen.

What does this mean? This means that I should be certain that these petitions are pleasing to our Father in heaven, and are heard by Him; for He Himself has commanded us to pray in this way and has promised to hear us. Amen, amen means "yes, yes, it shall be so."

Heavenly Father, teach me to say the "Amen" to my prayers. "Amen" means "true; it shall be so." "Amen" is the word of faith, so teach me to receive Your Word and promises with the "Amen" of faith, to acknowledge You as the Giver of all good gifts and to say with boldness and confidence, "Amen," that is, "It shall be so; Your gifts are received!" Only such a faith which trusts in You, given by the Holy Spirit, will encourage me to pray, to call upon You in every trouble and give You thanks and praise. Even though You have commanded me to pray, my sinful flesh does not want to. For Jesus' sake, who even during His greatest suffering did not fail to cry out to You, forgive me for my coldness in prayer, my lack of interest in taking Your Word upon my lips, and my indifference to crying out to You for all that I need for myself and others. Forgive me, Father, for disobeying Your command to pray and for not believing that You hear and answer my prayers!

Stir me up to prayer, Father, by that promise You have given to hear me when I pray. Let me approach You as children approach their fathers to ask for the things they need. Teach me to so trust in Your Word and promises that I cling to You in my prayers, crying out for all good and blessing from Your fatherly hand. Teach me to pray as Abraham, who was so bold as to intercede for Lot who was living in sinful Sodom. Teach me to pray as Jacob who wrestled with You and prevailed, not letting go until he received Your blessing. Teach me to pray as Moses who called You to repent of destroying Your people and instead to spare them for the sake of Your Name and promise. Teach me to pray as David and Solomon, seeking

Your wisdom and guidance. Teach me to cry out to You as the prophets did, who were surrounded by corruption and danger and yet trusted in Your Word. Teach me to pray with all boldness as even Your own Son prayed, entrusting Himself to Your will and care. Teach me to pray as the apostles and saints of the New Testament, who called upon You and patiently bore all things for the glory of Jesus' Name. Teach me, Father, to pray that way, with all boldness and confidence, trusting in Your promises.

Teach me to pray so that I learn what prayer is. Guard me from every temptation to think that You will only hear my prayer if I use the right words or the right amount of words. Guard me also from the evil notion that You will not hear my prayers unless enough people are praying. After all, Your apostle has written that the prayer of even one righteous man, which is what I am in Jesus Christ, avails much. Keep me also from vain babbling, Father. Let Your clear and direct Word of promise and blessing be the basis of my prayers. Let my words be the words of Jesus, the best words for my prayers, for how can You deny Your own Son? By the Holy Spirit, let me meditate upon the words of the prayer that He taught me, so that I may learn what Your will toward me is, and that I may learn what to believe, what to ask for, and what enemies there are from which I need You to defend me. And always, Lord, let me remember that when I am weak in my prayers, when they falter, and when I fail to pray, let me remember that the Spirit Himself cries out for me in words and groanings I don't even know. Comfort me also with Your Son's promise that He Himself intercedes for me before Your throne of grace. By these promises, stir me up to open my mouths in prayer and petitions, calling upon You without ceasing.

Hear my prayer, Father, for all those in need, especially *(names)*. When their suffering and circumstances cause their prayers to fail, then hear and answer my prayers on their behalf. Teach them through Your Word the command and promise to pray that in the midst of their struggles they too may know the comfort of Your good and gracious will. Put Your words upon their lips as they cry out to You and grant them whatever healing, comfort, and peace will restore and refresh them. And now, heavenly Father, having called upon You for all things, having put into Your ears the words of Your Son which He put upon my lips, now I end with the word of faith: "Amen." Now, Lord, as You have said and promised, so shall it be. Grant me faith to believe Your Word and promises always. In the Name of Jesus, who taught me to ask all things in His Name, I say: "Amen, Amen, yes, yes it shall be so."

First: What is Baptism?

Baptism is not just plain water, but it is the water included in God's command and combined with God's word.

Which is that word of God?

Christ our Lord says in the last chapter of Matthew: "Therefore go and make disciples of all nations, baptizing them in the name of the Father and of the Son and of the Holy Spirit." (Matthew 28:19)

From the beginning of time, O Lord, You have attached Your Word to the things of this world for the benefit and blessing of Your people. You once promised that by the Tree of Life, man would live forever, but, since I have fallen into sin, I have forfeited that gift of Eden. Nevertheless, in Your unceasing grace and mercy, You have given Your promise and blessing with so many earthly things that I can scarcely count them. I recall Your gracious promise to Noah of salvation from the Flood by means of the Ark. I remember the rod of Moses by which You parted the waters of the Red Sea to rescue Your people and to destroy their enemies. By the offerings of the Old Testament, You pointed the faithful to the promise of salvation in Your Son and by the blood of those offerings You accounted their sins forgiven, for Jesus' sake. By the waters of the Jordan You promised and gave healing to Naaman's leprosy. By the oil of anointing You set Your Word and promise upon prophets like Samuel and kings like David. Your Word was joined to the cross when the Word-made-flesh, the Son of God, was crucified for me, so that the Word and promise of the cross would be proclaimed until Jesus comes again. By His own Word, my Lord Jesus has established the promises of His Holy Sacraments. From His side flowed blood and water and those gifts are now given to the Church for the forgiveness of sins.

As I meditate upon the gift of Holy Baptism, let me rejoice that because this is no ordinary or plain water, but water which has Your command, it is a life-giving water. There is the temptation, Lord, to think that because my Baptism may have happened long ago or because it looks merely like just plain water, that Holy Baptism is no great gift. Forgive me for ever thinking such a thing! Forgive every denial of Your Word that Baptism is Your work. Teach me, Lord, that Baptism is not a human work, a sign or symbol of something in me, or a testimony about me. Teach me from Your Word how Holy Baptism is Your work, accomplished by Your Word through Your called minister. Teach me to look upon Baptism as it is, a holy and saving gift by which I am given Your Name and Your Word, the benefits of Christ's death for me, and by which I am rescued from sin and death.

When I am troubled by my enemies, the devil, the world, and my sinful nature, teach me to look outside myself to the sure rock and anchor of Holy Baptism. Since nothing is stronger than Your Word, and because Baptism has Your Word attached to it, teach me to look to my Baptism as a sure and certain comfort against all my enemies that seek to puff me up with self-righteousness or lead me down into the depths of despair. Rather let me look to my Baptism to see that, by that washing of water and the Word, I have a heavenly Father who will never forsake me, the true righteousness of the Son who lived and died and rose for me, and the peace and comfort of the Holy Spirit who was given to me just as He came down upon Jesus in the Jordan River. Here, Lord, I pray for all those who are troubled by sickness and other trials, especially *(names)*. Let them also be protected from despair by looking to the promise of their Baptism. Teach them as You do me that by this holy water and Word, I am united to Christ and therefore all that He has is now ours. Let us learn, Lord, that when we are troubled by the things of this life, to cry out: "But I am baptized! And if I am baptized, it is promised to me that I shall be saved and have eternal life, both in soul and body!" That, Lord, is to live in Your baptismal promises to me in Jesus.

Even as I trust in Baptism for the forgiveness of sins in this life, let me also be mindful of that promise that my Baptism into Christ means being united with His death and resurrection and His promise that He will raise me up on the Last Day. As I was born into this world in the natural way, already on my way to death, so comfort me that by my being born from above at the font, I am born now to eternal and everlasting life in

Christ Jesus. In Baptism, Lord, You have worked a holy work, accomplished a saving miracle, and delivered to me all that Christ accomplished on the cross, by the water that flowed from His pierced side, a refreshing stream into the holy font for my sake. I thank You, most holy Triune God, that You have put Your Name upon me with such an unshakeable and everlasting promise as the water and Word of my Baptism. Let me ever live by that holy water and Word so that my life may bring glory to You, Father, Son and Holy Spirit, one God now and forever. Amen.

Second: What benefits does Baptism give?

It works forgiveness of sins, rescues from death and the devil, and gives eternal salvation to all who believe this, as the words and promises of God declare.

Which are these words and promises of God?

Christ our Lord says in the last chapter of Mark: "Whoever believes and is baptized will be saved, but whoever does not believe will be condemned." (Mark 16:16)

Lord Jesus Christ, by the Word and water of Holy Baptism, Your victory has become mine. By this Holy Sacrament, the Spirit has bestowed upon me what You won for me on the cross of Calvary. I give You thanks for the powerful gifts and promises of my Baptism. I pray that You would help me to rightly consider my Baptism as the holy and saving gift that it is. Forgive me, Lord, for seeing my enemies and thinking I must fight them myself—as if I had the power to do so! Forgive me for forgetting or ignoring or despising the gifts You have given by this holy washing. Give me always faith in You and faith in my Baptism, that rejoicing in its holy gifts, I might live daily in Your holy faith. Guard me from every temptation to unbelief in which I would despise my Baptism, and even worse, sin in unbelief, deliberately and without repentance, thus condemning myself! From such a fate preserve me, dear Lord! Rather teach me always by Your Word and Spirit to know and believe that by trusting in the gifts of my Baptism, I am trusting in You and Your work of salvation.

I know many of my sins, and I know that I have many sins I do not know. I am born into this world corrupt and dying because of the curse of sin and the sin that has clung to me since the moment of my conception. I neither love God nor my neighbor as Your holy commandments teach me to do. I am self-centered and surround myself with idols, lusting after the things of this world. I, who am by nature sinful and unclean, am born into death. But in Baptism You have given me new life! I have been born again, from above, by the water and the Spirit at the font. Therefore, for the sake of Your own blood, sprinkled upon me in the waters of Baptism, forgive me all my sinfulness and every sin which I have committed or will commit. Cancel the curse that is upon me and wipe away the memory of every wicked thought, word and deed. When my sins trouble me, remind me of my Baptism that I may know that, for Your sake, my sins have been removed as far as the east is from the west. Comfort me with the promise of Baptism which clothes me with Your holiness and righteousness and makes my sins, which are scarlet, as white as snow! Teach me to rejoice and be glad that my Baptism is a heavenly flood, a gracious washing away of my iniquity, so that I might always stand before You with a clean conscience.

Lord, the enemies of death and the devil are constantly assaulting me. I am troubled by the approach of death. I am surrounded by death's work on those I know and love who have died. I tremble in fear over the passing away of this life. Let the promise of my Baptism rescue me from the despair and sadness of death! When I fear death, recall to my mind the holy promise that those who are baptized are saved, that by this washing of water and the Spirit I have new life and will be raised up on the Last Day. When death confronts me, let me hold before it my Baptism as a shield against its terror. Let me rejoice, on account of Your promise, that I who have been born from above and filled with Your Spirit will be raised up on the Last Day.

You know, Lord Jesus, the tempting power of the evil one, for You overcame his lies in the wilderness and upon the cross You snatched away his power and might forever. The devil attacks me relentlessly, tempting me to sin and trying to drag me away from You in despair and unbelief and by other great shame and vice. Therefore, Lord Jesus Christ, when the devil attacks, let me cling to my Baptism by which he might be driven away from me. My Baptism into the Triune name is Your own proof to Satan that he has no more claim on me: I am Yours! My Baptism is the testimony of God Himself that I will not be condemned for my sins but have been set free from them. Therefore, Satan has nothing with which to accuse me before Your throne! Keep me, then, safe in my Baptism from the evil one so that he may never cause me harm or danger. Whatever mischief and wickedness he seeks to accomplish upon me, let me fear nothing, but be confident in what You have made me and given me by the water and the Spirit.

To rescue me from sin, death, and the devil is to give me nothing else than eternal salvation. Grant me, Lord Jesus, through Your Holy Spirit, such confidence and trust in what You give me through Holy Baptism that I may confidently and boldly confess that it is Baptism which saves me. It is Baptism by which I am born again and born from above. It is Baptism which stands as Your own holy work upon me whereby I am made a child of God and received into Your holy kingdom. It is Baptism which enables me to say with confidence that I shall be raised on the Last Day and have everlasting life with You. Forgive me, Lord, for ever doubting this. Protect me from every sinful thought which would deny the power of Baptism and thereby deny Your Word. Let me never doubt my Baptism but live gladly and joyfully in it!

Finally, gracious Lord, let the same promises of Baptism which comfort me also bring comfort to those who suffer and have any particular need. Here I remember *(names)*. Let them, too, never fail of trusting in the promises of their Baptism so that in the midst of their struggles, temptations, and crosses, they may have joy and confidence in Your holy promises. Let them realize the solid rock upon which they stand in Holy Baptism. Let them know that You are with them because Your holy Name has been put upon them. Let them never doubt Your promise that they are Your precious children who have been born from above in this Holy Sacrament. Lord, I ask that You keep me in this holy baptismal faith until the day when You return to receive Your holy Bride, the Church, adorned and dressed beautifully, washed and prepared at the font for Your arrival; for Your live and reign with the Father and the Holy Spirit, one God, now and forever. Amen.

Third: How can water do such great things?

> *Certainly not just water, but the word of God in and with the water does these things, along with the faith which trusts this word of God in the water. For without God's word the water is plain water and no Baptism. But with the word of God it is a Baptism, that is, a life-giving water, rich in grace, and a washing of the new birth in the Holy Spirit, as St. Paul says in Titus, chapter three: "He saved us through the washing of rebirth and renewal by the Holy Spirit, whom He poured out on us generously through Jesus Christ our Savior, so that, having been justified by His grace, we might become heirs having the hope of eternal life. This is a trustworthy saying." (Titus 3:5–8)*

Heavenly Father, water is Your gift of life. Without it I would wither and perish. Without it the fruits of the earth would not blossom and provide for my daily bread. The water of Baptism is especially powerful because it has Your Word attached, Your command added, Your promise included. By this holy washing You have given me the new birth from above so that I may truly be called a child of God. By this Holy Sacrament You have renewed me by Your Holy Spirit from the corrupt ways of my former life. By Baptism I know that I am justified and stand righteous before You in Jesus Christ. By Baptism I know that an eternal and imperishable inheritance has been prepared for me and awaits me on the day my Lord returns in glory. Teach me to trust these promises of Baptism that the Spirit has given to me by the pen of the holy Apostle so that I might never doubt what my Baptism is and gives and does.

Protect me, Lord, from a superstitious trust in my Baptism. Guard me from a false faith which trusts in the outward action disconnected from Christ and His Word. Let me never fall into the sort of believing that trusts in Baptism as some "magical" act that will somehow save me while I despise it in a life of unrepentant sin! Keep me from rejecting Your gift that way! Rather, let me embrace my Baptism as the real and true delivery of all that You have promised in Jesus Christ. Grant me, by the Holy Spirit, to have faith that clings to and trusts in the Word and water together, confessing the forgiveness of sins and new life which Baptism gives me. Teach me true repentance each day so that I may live as those who are baptized, that is, walking in newness of life, not in the old ways of my slavery to sin.

Lord, grant me Your Holy Spirit also so that I may rightly confess the truth of my Baptism against all error. Never allow me to think that Baptism is merely an outward act or a human action. Let me never believe that Baptism is just a symbol or demonstration of something in me, my faith or decision or choice. Rather, strike such thinking from my mind and heart and teach me the true confession: that Baptism is YOUR work, done with the water You have created and the Word You have spoken, delivered by the mouth and hands of Your called and ordained servant, so that I may be certain my sins are forgiven and that I am Your child in Christ. Protect me, Lord, from the devil's lies about Baptism. Remind me that because it is Your Word that gives Baptism its power, I don't need to be baptized again and again. Your Word confesses "One Lord, one faith, one Baptism." So let me not seek other baptisms but give me faith to trust in the one Baptism of water and the Word that You have already given me. Rescue me also from any notion that I must add something to my Baptism to make it complete.

Heavenly Father, keep me from turning away from my Baptism, from denying it, or rejecting it or living as if I am not baptized and are not Your child. Your Word and promise are sure, but many drift away and do not live in that faith and promise. Hear my prayers for those who have done so, who have forgotten or outright denied what You have given them in Baptism. Here I ask You to remember *(names)*. Hear my prayer on their behalf and turn their hearts once again to rejoice in and trust in the salvation of Christ which was given them in their Baptism.

Against all the suffering and trials of this world, let my Baptism rescue me. I pray for those who are sick, suffering, near death, or in any trial and tribulation, especially *(names)*. Hear my prayer for them also that by the promises of their Baptism of new life and an eternal inheritance, they would be comforted against all adversity and difficulty. When these assaults bring them down, let me be Your faithful comforter by reminding them of what their Baptism gives them in Christ so that they may be spared any despair or misery. Rather, lift them up by the hope of that eternal inheritance which You have promised to all those who are born from above by water and the Spirit at Your holy font. Lord, You have joined Your Word to water to make a Baptism, a life-giving washing of grace. Hear my thanks and praise for this unbreakable gift, and may I always rejoice to know that to be baptized is to be in Christ Jesus. Hear me for the sake of His holy Name, put upon me with Yours and the Holy Spirit's on the day You marked me as Your own at the holy font. Amen.

Fourth: What does such baptizing with water indicate?

It indicates that the Old Adam in us should by daily contrition and repentance be drowned and die with all sins and evil desires, and that a new man should daily emerge and arise to live before God in righteousness and purity forever.

Where is this written?

St. Paul writes in Romans chapter six: "We were therefore buried with Him through baptism into death in order that, just as Christ was raised from the dead through the glory of the Father, we too may live a new life." (Romans 6:4)

Lord God, heavenly Father, I come before You afflicted by my sinful nature. Wherever there is temptation to deny You and serve myself, the Old Adam rushes in! He is always waiting to let my idolatry, greed, envy, lust, murder, and every other sin come out and be accomplished. He gladly lets the devil and the world stir up my thoughts to sinful things, and he delights in carrying out the wicked thoughts of my heart. Wherever I go, Father, I cannot avoid my Old Adam. I cannot get away from him. I cannot overcome him. I cannot defeat him. I cannot battle him alone. He runs wild with the devil and the world to lead me into sin and away from You. I cry out with St. Paul, that the good I want to do, I don't do, and the evil I don't want to do, that I do! Rescue me, Father, from this hideous enemy who lives inside me!

But You have rescued me! You have given me the victory in Christ Jesus. You buried me with Christ by my Baptism. In the water and the Word of the holy font, You have drowned that evil and sinful nature and raised up a new man in me. In Baptism, by being in Christ, You have made me a new creation in Jesus. My rescue from the Old Adam is that he is crucified with my Lord and I am raised from the dead with Jesus. In my Baptism You have given me the Holy Spirit to battle against my sinful flesh, to preserve me from his lusts and evil thoughts and actions, and to keep me, by Your Word and Sacraments, in Christ.

All this You have done for me by Your grace and mercy in Jesus Christ. Yet this battle is a daily battle in which my Old Adam fights against the New Man. The sinful nature, which You drowned by water and the Spirit, continues to rise up and try his old tricks again. He never stops trying to drag me away from the Faith and to stop me from doing anything good for my neighbor. Therefore, heavenly Father, continue to strengthen me by Your Word that I may, each day by daily contrition and repentance, drown the Old Adam with all his sins and evil desires. Teach me contrition, Lord. Teach me to fear my sins. To fear offending Your majesty. To despise my sins and sinfulness. Teach me to be truly sorry for the things I have done to dishonor You and hurt and harm my neighbor. Stir up within me true sorrow and horror for every thought, word, and deed that is against Your will and contrary to Your holy Commandments. The Old Adam wants to rejoice and be happy in my sins. Let it never be, dear Lord, but let me drown him with true sorrow over them. Let me also by true repentance push him back into the drowning waters of my Baptism. Teach me true repentance, to turn from and flee from my sins and to trust that, in Christ, my sins are truly forgiven. With sins forgiven, the Old Adam has nothing to cling to and Satan has no evidence against me.

Also, Lord, my Baptism has made me into a new creation. You have raised me with Christ to live a new life, a life in which my heart, soul, and strength are given in love to You and my life is given in service to my neighbor. Teach me, by my Baptism, that my salvation is not just for my own sake, not just to rescue me from my sins, but rather it causes You to work through me such works as will be a help and blessing to others. By Your Word and Spirit, given in Your Church through Your Means of Grace, stir up in me a true and holy love of You, Your Name, and Your Word. Create in me a clean heart and renew that right Spirit within me that looks to You for all my good and comfort and that offers every good work and comfort to those around me. Make my life truly one that is new, separated from the sinful nature's old ways of godlessness and selfishness. Turn my heart to You and to the good of my neighbor that the world may see my good works and give glory to You, my Father in heaven. And in this new life which You give and renew in me each day, keep my hope and faith and trust always in the waters of my Baptism, which means, in Christ, as my Savior from all sin and death and the One who has defeated my Old Adam once and for all. Lift up my heart to long for that blessed day when my Lord returns in glory and I am raised up from the dead sinless and pure and righteous forever and ever with You.

Lord, hear my prayer also for all those whose battle with the Old Adam is bitter and hard. Hear my prayers, for the sake of their Baptism into Christ, for all those who struggle with particular sins and sorrows. Especially hear my prayer for *(names)*. Comfort them and strengthen them in their Baptism. Let them too, by the power of Your Holy Spirit, learn contrition and repentance. Sustain their faith in Christ and let them never fail to know the victory over sin that is theirs by the Spirit who dwells in them, delivering them daily from their sinful flesh and renewing their New Man in Christ. Let them never be separated from Your Word and Gifts lest their sinful nature gain the upper hand and pull them away from Christ. Be their strong shield and sure defense against whatever would harm them. Finally, let them look with hope to the coming eternity of righteousness and purity they will share with Christ their Savior.

At the font, O Triune God, Father, Son and Holy Spirit, You descended and came to me, marking me as Your own and saving me from the kingdom of the evil one. Now grant that in my life my Baptism and new life will be evident to all. Keep me and all Your baptized children safe in Christ Jesus until He comes again in His glory to complete and establish me in the work that began that day at Your holy font. Hear this prayer for the sake of Christ, in whose Name this Baptized child of Yours prays. Amen.

What is Confession?

Confession has two parts. First, that we confess our sins, and second, that we receive absolution, that is, forgiveness, from the pastor as from God Himself, not doubting, but firmly believing that by it our sins are forgiven before God in heaven.

Merciful Lord, the Holy Spirit has written through the Apostle that if I confess my sin, You are faithful and just to forgive my sins and cleanse me from all unrighteousness. Teach me not to deny that I am sinful and daily sin, lest I be a liar in Your sight. Rather, by Your holy Law, open my eyes and heart to the truth and horror of my sinful nature and my sins both against You and against others. Teach me to examine myself to see where I have missed the mark, fallen short, and trespassed against Your holy commandments. Even more, teach me true contrition and repentance so that I see my sins and flee from them, mourn them, hate them, and desire them to be forgiven. Turn my heart in faith and trust to Christ's word of forgiveness spoken to me by my fellow Christians and especially by my pastor who speaks in Christ's place.

Forgive me, Lord, for hanging on to sins as if I could get rid of them myself. When miserable Judas betrayed Your Son, he fled to the religious men and they told him to see to it himself. Rescue me from any desire or attempt to deal with my own sins, thinking that I could get rid of them or make up for them by what I do. Grant me true repentance, which is to turn from my sins to the free and complete forgiveness bestowed upon me by Your crucified and risen Son. Stir up my heart to confess my sins to You and to those against whom I have sinned. Do not leave me in the darkness of the lie that I am not too sinful or that I am a pretty good person. By Your Word, which is a two-edged sword, pierce me to heart and marrow that I may know my sins and flee from them to Christ. Remove from me every fear of confessing my sins, admitting I have done wrong to those whom I hurt, and let me humbly seek their forgiveness in Christ.

Also, my pastor *(father confessor)* has been given to me by you, Lord, to hear my confession and to absolve me. Let me rejoice in the words that he speaks in the stead and by the command of Christ. Enable me to firmly and truly believe that his forgiveness is Your forgiveness. Stir up my heart also to seek out my pastor *(father confessor)* for those sins which particularly trouble and burden me. Take from me all fear about baring my soul and heart to the shepherd whom You have appointed to absolve me of my sins. Remind me that it is my pastor's *(father confessor's)* delight to pronounce to me the saving words of Absolution and declare, by Christ's command, that my sins are forgiven. Holy Spirit, fill my pastor *(father confessor)* with the strength to bear these burdens of sins which he hears and the power to faithfully hold sacred the seal of confession, never revealing to anyone what has been confessed and is buried now in Christ's tomb. Let the words of Absolution be my comfort and joy against all sin and the attacks of the devil who would accuse me on the basis of my sin. Let me rejoice in the freedom from such accusation that the words of Holy Absolution deliver!

(For Pastors)

Lord Jesus Christ, You have called me and set me into the Office of the Holy Ministry for the purpose of absolving sinners who are troubled and burdened by their iniquities. Make me Your faithful servant to hear their confession and to pronounce forgiveness in Your name. As I hear the sins that trouble Your people, put upon my lips Your holy words of comfort. Help me in directing them to the comfort and wisdom of the Holy Scriptures. Let me assure them of Your mercy and give them godly advice and counsel according to Your Word. Grant me to faithfully absolve them and declare their sins forgiven for Christ's sake, delivering not my forgiveness but what is truly and rightly Your own forgiveness. Grant me Your Holy Spirit that I may faithfully carry the burdens of my brothers and sisters and hold sacred and inviolate the holy seal of confession. Rescue me from every temptation to reveal what has been confessed or to act toward them on the basis of their sins! May it never be, O Lord! Rather, by Your grace and mercy, teach me to forget and bury this confession and always to look upon Your forgiven saints as holy and righteous in You, just as my Father in heaven beholds them!

+   +   +

Many of my brothers and sisters in the faith are troubled by their sins, O Lord. Some are burdened by what they have said, thought or done and others have fallen into sin and do not recognize their iniquity. Here I remember *(names)*. For those who are burdened, help me to faithfully proclaim Christ and His forgiveness to them and encourage them to receive Holy Absolution from their pastor. For those who are in some sin, enable me to speak the truth in love, urging them to repentance and faith in Christ's promises. Teach me also personally never to reveal a confidence but make me faithful in urging upon them Your Word and its call to repentance and faith in Jesus Christ.

Now, Lord, free of the shackles of my sins by the word of Absolution, having returned to the waters of Baptism by confessing my sins and being absolved, let me live now in peace. Let no sins trouble me. Do not let the devil bind my conscience or accuse me. By Your promise that all is forgiven, teach me to live now every day for Your glory and the good of my neighbor. Hear my prayer now in the Name of Your Son Jesus Christ whose beautiful feet bring the Good News of peace with You through the forgiveness He won for me on Calvary. Amen.

What sins should I confess?

Before God we should plead guilty of all sins, even those we are not aware of, as we do in the Lord's Prayer; but before the pastor we should confess only those sins which we know and feel in our hearts.

Which are these?

Consider your place in life according to the Ten Commandments: Are you a father, mother, son, daughter, husband, wife, or worker? Have you been disobedient, unfaithful, or lazy? Have you been hot-tempered, rude, or quarrelsome? Have you hurt someone by your words or deeds? Have you stolen, been negligent, wasted anything, or done any harm?

Heavenly Father, hear my plea for Your mercy and the forgiveness of sins. You know my every sin of thought, word, and deed, even those I have forgotten and do not know. If you, Lord, kept a record of my sins, who could stand? Who could face You? But with You there is forgiveness, therefore You are feared. With You there is forgiveness for the sake of Your Son's sacrifice for sinners on the cross. Forgive me, therefore, Lord, of every thought, word, and deed that is against Your will, in which I have not loved You and have not loved my neighbor. Grant me comfort against the accusations of Satan and my own conscience. Let me never believe the lie that because I have sinned, You will not forgive or receive me. Against that lie, let the truth of the Gospel stand firm. Indeed, Lord, my sins deserve Your punishment. Nevertheless, Jesus has carried my sins, taken the blame, suffered Your judgment so that now I am free. Still, Lord, there are times when a particular sin troubles me. I hear Your forgiveness, but I still suffer the weight and burden of the guilt of something I have done against You or my neighbor. When I suffer such a weight of sin, remind me that You have given me a pastor whose job it is to hear my confession of such sin and pronounce absolution, specifically and graciously for such sins that trouble me. Teach me not to fear my pastor but to hear from him the holy and comforting words of Jesus against all my sins. Let him declare to me, as Your messenger and ambassador, Your holy will: that my sins are blotted out in Christ!

As I meditate upon the words of the Catechism, I see that in my various callings, I have fallen far short of Your glory. Hear my confession for such sins.

(OF PARENTS)

Lord, You have given to me the blessing of children. I so often take them for granted! Forgive me for neglecting them in any way, for being impatient and irritated with them. Forgive me when I am too harsh with them, when I exasperate and trouble them. Forgive me when I am too lenient, neglecting my holy duty to correct and even punish them. Forgive me for not encouraging them in the faith and for despising and not fulfilling the promises I made at their Baptism. Forgive me for not spending adequate time with them, for not counseling them and giving them wisdom as they grow up. Forgive me for ever despising my children or being angry with them for selfish reasons. Remind me, Lord, through Your Word and Spirit, that even as I am Your child in Christ and You are my Father in heaven, that for the sake of my brother, Jesus Christ, all these sins are wiped away and do not stand against me. Create a clean heart in me, O God, and renew a right Spirit within me so that I may faithfully carry out this holy calling You have given me.

(OF CHILDREN)

Heavenly Father, You are my Father in and through Jesus Christ. Forgive me for every sin against my earthly parents. Forgive me for thinking I know more than they do and for questioning their guidance and wisdom. Forgive me for back-talking, disobeying, and dishonoring them. Forgive me for failing to do what they ask and for doing what they tell me not to do. No matter how old I am, my sinful flesh still rebels against the authority of my father and mother! Forgive me for hating them, wishing I was away from them, and for failing to see that they stand in Your place on this earth to provide and care for me. Forgive me for taking them for granted and for failing to thank You for their care and provision. Forgive me for not praying for them and asking Your blessings and benefits upon their difficult task of raising me! Remind me, Lord, through Your Word and Spirit, that even as I am Your child and owe You as my heavenly Father all thanks and praise, that I owe my parents also my honor and love and obedience. Create in me a clean heart, O God, and renew a right Spirit within me so that I may faithfully live as Your child and theirs, honoring my father and mother in all things.

(OF HUSBANDS AND WIVES)

Lord, graciously hear my prayer for mercy. In Christ, forgive me all my sins against my *husband/wife*. Forgive me for selfishness and for neglecting *his/her* needs. Forgive me for putting myself first and for being inconsiderate. Forgive me for not helping *him/her* in my family life as I should, letting *him/her* unequally bear the burden and load of my household. Forgive me for hurtful words and actions and for the terrible transgression of bringing up *his/her* past sins. Forgive me for failing to forgive my *husband/wife* and instead bearing ill will, holding a grudge, and letting anger and hatred cling to me. Forgive me, Lord, for adulterous thoughts, words, and deeds by which I despise and dishonor my spouse and seek pleasure or contentment outside of the bounds of marriage. Forgive me for failing to lift up, extol, speak well of, defend, honor, and cherish my *husband/wife* as I should. Remind me, by Your Word and Spirit, that Christ has given Himself for His Church, His holy Bride, and that this holy mystery is also what is to be pictured by my marriage. Create in me a clean heart, O God, and renew a right Spirit within me so that I may act as a faithful and Christian spouse in all things, to Your glory and the joy and happiness of the one whom You have given me as a companion for this life.

+   +   +

Heavenly Father, in all my life, forgive me every sin, which is against You and every person, in every calling of mine. Forgive me for dishonoring authority, wasting time at school or on the job. Forgive me for grumbling and complaining, for insulting and belittling. Forgive me for doubt and worry, rashness and anger. Forgive me for neglecting Your Word and misusing Your Name, especially by not calling upon it. Have mercy upon me and forgive every sin of speaking badly about and against others, of coveting and being dissatisfied with whatever You have given me. Forgive me also for *(particular sins may be mentioned here)*. In short, O Lord, blot out my every transgression and iniquity for the sake of Jesus Christ. Turn my heart in faith to the promises of Holy Baptism, Absolution, and the Body and Blood of Christ, all of which are given to take away my sins. Comfort me against every burden of conscience and fiery dart of Satan's accusations. Let me believe only Your Word, that for Christ's sake I am forgiven. And, having forgiven me, Lord, stir up in me the desire to turn from my sins, to amend my life, and to live for Your glory and the blessing of those around me. Again, Lord, I remember those who are troubled by or caught in some sin, especially *(names)*. Rescue them also by Your Word of forgiveness. Turn their hearts in true repentance to faith in Christ. For this purpose Your Son came into this world: to accomplish for me the forgiveness of sins. For this purpose You have brought me into the church: to bestow upon me that forgiveness. Let me live in it each day, acknowledging my wrong and rejoicing in the forgiveness given to me by Jesus Christ, in His Name I pray. Amen.

What is the Office of the Keys?

The Office of the Keys is that special authority which Christ has given to His church on earth to forgive the sins of repentant sinners, but to withhold forgiveness from the unrepentant as long as they do not repent.

Where is this written?

This is what St. John the Evangelist writes in chapter twenty: The Lord Jesus breathed on His disciples and said, "Receive the Holy Spirit. If you forgive anyone his sins, they are forgiven; if you do not forgive them, they are not forgiven." (John 20:22–23)

What do You believe according to these words?

I believe that when the called ministers of Christ deal with us by His divine command, in particular when they exclude openly unrepentant sinners from the Christian congregation and absolve those who repent of their sins and want to do better, this is just as valid and certain, even in heaven, as if Christ our dear Lord dealt with us Himself.

Lord Jesus Christ, how will I know what You have done for me unless You declare it to me? How will I have the forgiveness You won for me bestowed upon me unless You send Your preachers to proclaim it? How shall I hear unless You send them so that, by the hearing of Your Word, I might have faith? When You forgave the sins of the paralytic, the crowds marveled that God had given such authority to men. Now, Lord, You have given that same authority to the men You call and ordain to be preachers so that they might comfort me with the forgiveness of sins. You have given that authority to all Your people so that I might comfort others and lift the burdens of sin that are upon my brothers and sisters in Christ. Teach me, Lord, to know I need such forgiveness, to cry out for Your mercy against my sins, and to receive the Holy Absolution with true faith in Your promises.

Lord, You do not leave me to the uncertain thoughts of my heart and mind. Rather, You send Your preachers into the world, calling them into service in Your Church so that, through an earthly and human voice, You may declare to me that my sins are no more. Forgive me, Lord, for despising or neglecting to seek Your comfort through the ministry of the pastor You have given to me. Forgive me, Lord, for taking lightly or not believing that my pastor's forgiveness is Your forgiveness. Since You have called him, he speaks not his own words but Your Word. Make him ever faithful in doing that! Guard me from falling into such sin that my pastor should ever have to bind my sins and shut Your kingdom to me! From this preserve me, O Lord! Rather, teach me to live so that my whole life will be a life of repentance, constantly seeking and hearing the Good News that my sins are forgiven. Teach me to believe the words of my pastor and to receive them with glad confidence, not as the words of a mere man but as Your own words that are upon his lips. Let me receive him as an ambassador and herald of the joyful pronouncement that You, my King, have put away all my sins and iniquities. Be with my pastor when he must confront the unrepentant. Let him take seriously his office of calling sinners to repentance. Open their hearts to turn from their sin and seek the good news of forgiveness. *(Here remember anyone who has been disciplined or excommunicated.)* Thank you, Lord Jesus, that You have breathed upon my pastor with Your Holy Spirit so that he may faithfully deliver to me what You have accomplished on Calvary.

(FOR PASTORS)

Lord, You have set Your Holy Spirit upon me in my ordination to be the voice that declares and proclaims the forgiveness of sins that You won for all people by Your death and resurrection. Make me a faithful minister of Your Word, never seeking my own glory but faithfully preaching and teaching Your Word and absolving sinners who repent. Give me strength, Lord, to confront anyone who is living in sin of which they will not repent. Put Your words upon my lips to call them to repentance, even unto binding their sins if need be. Open their hearts so that Your

Word may turn them from sin and death to faith in You and life everlasting. Here, Lord, I remember those who need to hear Your call to repentance from their sins, *(especially names)*. Here also, I pray for those who struggle with their sins, *(especially names)* that they may be comforted by the Absolution I pronounce to them. Help me distinguish between hard hearts and those who have stumbled so that I may never, as You never, break a bruised reed or quench a smoldering wick. Help me, as Your minister, to speak the truth in love. Let me never forget that I am speaking not for myself but for You, that I may do so faithfully and for the comfort of troubled sinners. Let Your people rejoice in the words I speak, receiving comfort from Your promises.

+   +   +

Lord, the world scoffs that a man can forgive sins. Many will claim that only God can forgive sins. Yet, Lord, on the day You rose from the grave, You breathed upon Your disciples and set them under orders to forgive and retain sins, speaking under Your own authority. Guard me from every false doctrine that seeks to take Your forgiveness out of the mouth of Your people. Protect me from every lie that says I must seek You alone for forgiveness and yet gives no way in which to hear and receive it. For how then will I know for certain my sins are forgiven, if not through the lips of another human being that You have given to speak my forgiveness? Stir me up, O Lord, to believe the words You have given Your pastors to speak and to seek out that comfort when my sins trouble my conscience.

Also, Lord Jesus, remind me that, since You have risen from the dead and my sins are gone, all Your people can forgive sins. Teach me, in my daily callings to speak forgiveness to those who sin against me and to tell them also that such forgiveness is theirs in Christ. Make me, in whom You live, a "little Christ" who bears witness to the world of the forgiveness of sins which You accomplished for all people. Lord, help me especially to forgive and set aside the sins of those who have hurt or angered me, *(especially names)*. As You have not held my sins against me, rescue me from holding someone else's sins against them, lest I cut off Your forgiveness and be filled with hatred instead of love. When I fail in my calling as a

Christian, let me never be afraid to seek out my pastor, confess my sins, and be comforted by Your Absolution through him. Thank you, Lord, for the gift of Your forgiveness, spoken by my pastor and other Christians. Thanks be to God for this holy gift which You have given Your Church. Let me always rejoice, Lord, that with these holy keys You have given to Your Church, the gates of heaven stand open to me that I may enter holy and clothed in Your righteousness. Hear my prayers for the sake of Your holy Name. Amen.

What is the Sacrament of the Altar?

It is the true body and blood of our Lord Jesus Christ under the bread and wine, instituted by Christ Himself for us Christians to eat and to drink.

Where is this written?

The holy Evangelists Matthew, Mark, Luke, and St. Paul write: Our Lord Jesus Christ, on the night when He was betrayed, took bread, and when He had given thanks, He broke it and gave it to the disciples and said: "Take, eat; this is My body, which is given for you. This do in remembrance of Me."

In the same way also He took the cup after supper, and when He had given thanks, He gave it to them, saying, "Drink of it, all of you; this cup is the new testament in My blood, which is shed for you for the forgiveness of sins. This do, as often as you drink it, in remembrance of Me."

Most holy and gracious Lord Jesus, You, who are true God and true man, have come into this world in the flesh, born of the Virgin, baptized with sinners, bearing the sins of the world as the Lamb of God. You carried my sins to Calvary, were betrayed by sinful men, judged by sinful men, condemned by sinful men, and crucified by sinful men. All this was done for all sinners. Without being asked, without being thanked, without expecting anything in return, You obeyed Your Father's will to suffer and die in my place. Your holy death is my salvation! Your innocent suffering and death is the ransom price You have offered to redeem me from the evil one. On the very night that Your holy suffering began, You gave to Your disciples this most precious gift: Your own Body and Blood to eat and drink. As the Passover Lamb of old was slaughtered and then eaten, so You, Lord Jesus, the Lamb of God who takes away the sin of the world, have been sacrificed for me on the cross and are now eaten in Your Holy Supper.

How could I ever know, Lord, that this death upon the cross is for me? How can I receive the forgiveness that Your death accomplished for sinners? How shall that blood which poured from Your side so long ago rescue me today from sin and death? You, Lord Jesus, having risen from the dead and ascended to the Father's right hand, now give me in Your Holy Supper Your own true Body and Blood that was sacrificed for me on the cross! Forgive me, Lord, should I ever doubt Your Word as to what I receive in the Holy Sacrament of Your Body and Blood. Rescue me from every lie that denies Your words and would see in this sacrament anything other than what You have said it to be. Protect me from those lies that teach me the bread and wine are just symbols of Your Body and Blood. Guard me from the false notion that the point of this meal is to somehow go up to You by faith because You are not really present in this Supper. Rather, confirm in me, by Your Holy Spirit, the faith which clings to Your Body and Blood truly present under the bread and wine for the forgiveness of my sins.

Jesus, Your own Words tell me why I need to eat and drink Your Body and Blood. You taught Your disciples that whoever eats Your flesh and drinks Your blood will live forever. Therefore, fortify and inoculate me against death with Your Body and Blood. It is indeed a 'medicine of immortality!' Your own Word says that, when I eat Your flesh and drink Your blood, You live in me and I in You, and You will raise me up on the Last Day. Therefore, when I receive Your Body and Blood, teach me to rejoice in Your triumph over death that is made ours by Your living in me. Teach me, Lord, to confidently confess that, by eating and drinking Your Body and Blood, my sins are truly and completely forgiven. Whenever my conscience troubles me, bring to mind what has been given in Your Supper. When my sins weigh me down, stir me up with a hunger and thirst for righteousness that is satisfied at Your altar where You feed me the righteousness of God, the forgiveness of sins through Your own Body and Blood.

The psalmist declares, "Taste and see that the Lord is good!" So I taste Your goodness when I eat and drink Your Body and Blood. You have given it for me as a Christian to eat and drink. Forgive me also, Lord, when I despise Your Word and invitation. When I grow cold and indifferent, with no hunger and thirst, rescue me by Your Word and Spirit, stirring up in me that holy desire to come to Your altar and be satisfied with Your goodness. Open my mouth, Lord, and fill it with Your gifts! Hear also my prayers for those who have neglected this gift and who, through the devil's working, have lost the desire to feast upon Your Body and Blood. Especially I pray for *(names)*. Teach me, as their *brother/sister* in Christ, to encourage them and remind them of the blessings You have for Christians at Your altar! I remember before You also, dear Savior, those who are ill, homebound, or for some other reason cannot be present with Your people when You gather them for worship, *(especially names)*. Grant my pastor to be faithful in visiting them and delivering Your Body and Blood for their comfort and strength. Then I shall rejoice to be united in one Holy Church, having eaten and drunk the same gifts from Your gracious hand!

Eye has not seen and ear has not heard, Lord, what You have in store for me in the glory that is to come! There shall be Your feast, the marriage feast of the Lamb, that cannot be described by my words! There shall be a feast on the mountain of the Lord where I eat and drink without money and without cost! Yet even now I enjoy the foretaste of this feast in Your Holy Supper. Even now I am joined with the saints and angels around Your throne in eternity. Even now You are present with me bodily in this Supper. Therefore, until the Father brings all things to completion on the Last Day, preserve me in Your body, the Church, by always feeding me Your Body and Blood. With You living in me and I in You, I look forward to the day when I shall overcome death by Your power and be raised up to life everlasting! I give You thanks, Lord Jesus Christ, for the gift of Your Body and Blood, for You, who feed me in this holy meal, yet live and reign with the Father and the Holy Spirit, one God, now and forever. Amen.

What is the benefit of this eating and drinking?

These words, "Given and shed for you for the forgiveness of sins," show us that in the Sacrament forgiveness of sins, life, and salvation are given us through these words. For where there is forgiveness of sins, there is also life and salvation.

Lord Jesus, who gave Yourself over into death at the hands of sinful men, You have secured my salvation. You have rescued me from the curse of the Law, the punishment of death, and the bonds of the evil one. Your death has taken away my sins. Every sin, transgression, iniquity, and trespass I have done and even the very original sin that infects me—all of this has been forgiven for Your sake. My sin is put away, cast into the depths of the sea, washed white by Your blood, pardoned, forgotten, no longer held against me, removed, wiped out. My sin is forgiven! And this, Lord, You grant me, not because of anything in myself, not by my deserving it, not by my working to earn it. It is mine by grace, through Your Word and Sacraments. Teach me, Lord, that this is what salvation means: that everything that once stood against me before God no longer condemns me. Teach me that, for Your sake, I may confidently confess, "My sins are forgiven!"

Yet, Lord, my conscience troubles me. I know my sins are forgiven. I have heard the words. Yet Satan still tries to trick me and tempt me to unbelief and despair. With the sins of my past and with recent sins, the evil one seeks to whisper to me that I am no Christian, no child of God, and deserving of nothing but hell and eternal misery. When my conscience troubles me, when Satan whispers at me, when the world sees and accuses me of hypocrisy, turn me to You, Lord. Turn me to seek Your altar and Your Body and Blood. There, with such strong words, "Given and shed for You for the forgiveness of sins," how can I doubt Your promise that You will never forsake me! By Your Body and Blood, You forgive my sins! Hear my prayer for mercy and once again have pity on me. Forgive and blot out all fear and distrust of Your Word. By the Body and Blood that You give me to eat and drink, forgive not only my doubts and fears but all my sins: every sin against You, Your Name, and Your Word; every sin against neighbor (parents and children, spouses, friends, and others). Where my conscience would convict me, let Your clear words, "Given and shed for You for the forgiveness of sins," echo in my heart and mind and thus drive away these lying spirits.

In this world of death, brought on by sin, teach me that Your forgiveness is life. The wages of sin is death, but, by forgiving my sins, You have gained me life. You even promise, Lord Jesus, that to feast upon Your flesh and blood means that You will raise me up on the Last Day. Therefore, by Your Holy Supper, rescue me from all fear of death. By Your Body and Blood, which has died and risen from death, rescue me from death itself and raise me up on that Last Day. As I walk through this valley of the shadow of death, make me to know that the forgiveness I receive at Your altar is my life. Teach me, Lord, that in the midst of death, I am alive in You because You live in me.

Then, Lord, protect me from all the false notions of "salvation" that are out there. I know, Lord, that I should strive, and do strive by Your Holy Spirit to live a better life—to love You more and to love others more. But do not let me make my salvation a matter of how well I'm doing at that! For if I were only saved because I have improved or changed, then I am surely doomed! Let me neither see my salvation as some work of my own, something I have done to earn a place with You. No, let me know that Your forgiveness is my salvation, and that it comes from You. When I think of my salvation and eternal life, when I want to see it, know I have it, be confident in it, then answer that prayer at Your altar. There, eating and drinking Your Body and Blood, grant me such a faith that confidently confesses against all evil and sin that I am saved and that You are my Savior. Then I shall know Your promise that nothing can snatch me from Your hand.

Your Words, "Given and shed for You for the forgiveness of sins," are an anchor against stormy seas, a shield against the poisonous arrows of the enemy, a light in the darkness, and a rock upon which to stand. With these words, the kingdom of Satan is thrown down, and I rise up in victory. With these Words of Yours, I overcome all sin, death, and condemnation, trading them for forgiveness, life, and salvation. Let this glad confidence and hope be for all Your people, Lord. Now hear my prayer for those who are in distress and need Your help and grace, *(especially names)*. Let those words of Yours, "given and shed for You for the forgiveness of sins," be their strength amid all adversity. Deliver to them Your Body and Blood also and let them draw their true comfort from You Word and Body and Blood. What sweet and holy gifts You give me by this Holy Supper, Lord! Let me never despise it but always with thanksgiving receive it joyfully! I praise and thank You for this holy gift and for the Words that deliver what they promise, for You indeed reign with the Father and the Holy Spirit, one God, now and forever. Amen.

How can bodily eating and drinking do such great things?

Certainly not just eating and drinking do these things, but the words written here: "Given and shed for you for the forgiveness of sins." These words, along with the bodily eating and drinking, are the main thing in the Sacrament. Whoever believes these words has exactly what they say: "forgiveness of sins."

Lord Jesus Christ, in the Divine Service of Your holy Church, by the holy mysteries of Your Word and Sacraments, You raise me up to seat me with You in the heavenly places. My feeble mind cannot grasp how it may be that, with bread and wine, You give to me Your Body and Blood to eat and drink. I should never believe such a thing according to the wisdom of this world, or science or reason or observation. Rather, I trust this promise because of Your Word that does what it says and gives what it says it gives. On the night of the Passover, Your people took a lamb and killed it and ate it, in anticipation of Your mighty deliverance. Now, You, Lord, the true Passover Lamb, have been slain on Calvary, and I feast upon Your flesh and blood. Here You are faithful to Your Word that declares that to eat Your flesh and drink Your blood is to have eternal life, and You will raise me up on the Last Day.

Lord, You would not give me this holy gift of Your Body and Blood for the forgiveness of sins if I didn't need such forgiveness! Therefore, teach me to know and acknowledge and confess my sins and iniquities rightly, trembling at my faults but yet rejoicing in their forgiveness by Your sacrifice on the cross that is delivered into my mouth in Your Holy Supper. Remind me, by Your Word, how I do not love God with my whole heart, soul, mind, and strength! Teach me how I fail to love my neighbor as myself. Call to mind my lack of hunger and thirst for Your righteousness and my coldness in desiring Your Body and Blood, as if they are optional or not important! By Your Holy Spirit, stir up in me a fervent longing and hunger and thirst for Your Body and Blood, knowing that by eating and drinking these, my sins are truly, fully, freely, and without question forgiven and blotted out. Teach me, by eating and drinking Your Body and Blood, that nothing stands between me and the Father and that I shall face no judgment for my sins because they have been forgiven.

Also, Lord, let me never separate the eating and drinking of Your Body and Blood from the forgiveness of sins. Let no thought of the devil, the world, or my sinful flesh come to me to fool me into believing that eating and drinking Your Body and Blood is unimportant or that I do not need it constantly! Stir up my heart to desire this holy gift whenever it is offered and never to despise it as if I somehow can be strong on my own without it, or that my sins are not so bad as to need it! Grant me, by the Holy Spirit, such true faith and trust in Your Words, "given and shed for You for the forgiveness of sins," that no doubt or temptation to unbelief can cause me to deny this gift! Let it be, Lord, that by faith I have exactly what Your Words say: the forgiveness of sins! Where my faith is weak, strengthen it so that, by Your Word and Body and Blood, I may be preserved from all false belief and always have comfort for my conscience when it is troubled by my sins.

Lord, there are many even who call themselves Christians who deny Your Words. They see the Sacrament of the Altar as nothing more than a symbol or ritual to be done with no benefits of forgiveness and comfort. Therefore, make me always bold to confess what it is that You give in this holy meal, namely, Your Body and Blood for the forgiveness of sins. Let me never think this is not an important distinction! Rather, with patience and love to my neighbor, help me to confess Your Word as You have given it, as something to be treasured because it brings such great comfort. Help me to show others that the strength and power of this sacrament are not in my feelings or my obedience but in Your Word, Your Body and Blood that are present, and Your promise of forgiveness, life, and salvation given here.

Finally, gracious Lord, let Your Words, "given and shed for you for the forgiveness of sins," be a comfort to those who are sick, who are suffering, who are troubled, who are faltering, who are weak, or whose sins trouble them greatly. Especially I ask for *(names)*, that Your Holy Supper be a comfort to them in their distress. Make my pastors faithful in bringing Your Word and Body and Blood to those who are not able to receive it with Your congregation. Bless Your ministers also in teaching Your people always to look away from themselves and to Your Body and Blood for forgiveness, life, salvation, comfort, hope, and true joy. The benefits, Lord Jesus, of eating Your Body and drinking Your Blood are given to me by Your Word. I give You thanks always for this most holy gift, Who lives and reigns with the Father and the Holy Spirit, one God, now and forever. Amen.

Who receives this Sacrament worthily?

Fasting and bodily preparation are certainly fine outward training. But that person is truly worthy and well prepared who has faith in these words: "Given and shed for you for the forgiveness of sins."

But anyone who does not believe these words or doubts them is unworthy and unprepared, for the words "for you" require all hearts to believe.

Gracious Lord Jesus, You have given Yourself to death for my sins, risen from the dead, and now come to me in Your Body and Blood to bestow upon me forgiveness of sins, life, and salvation. When I come into Your presence, I bow before my King. Yet I am not worthy to approach You. I should stand far off and not even lift up my head. I should stay at a distance and cry out, "Unclean!" as the lepers once did. Yet it is not any worthiness in me that makes me prepared to receive Your Body and Blood. It is Your gracious invitation to sinners to eat and drink these holy gifts precisely to forgive me my sins. My worthiness is not in anything I have done, but it is in Your holy obedience to the Father. By Your perfection bestowed upon me in Baptism and Your Word, You Yourself have become my worthiness by which I may open my mouth to eat and drink Your holy Body and Blood. For this I give You thanks and praise, for how else should I come except that You Yourself have invited me to this Feast, and You Yourself have clothed me so that I should be prepared to receive it.

Forgive me, Lord, for thinking that I come to Your altar because of some worthiness in me. Forgive me for thinking that because I am a member of a particular church or because I have studied the Catechism and been confirmed that I have some "right" to receive Your Body and Blood. Forgive me for any idea that it doesn't matter what a person believes when they receive Your Holy Supper. Forgive me for desiring forgiveness for myself when I would hold someone else's sins against them. Forgive me for not rightly examining myself before I eat and drink Your Body and Blood, receiving it as if I don't really need or don't really care about the gift given, the forgiveness of sins. Forgive me, Lord, for every thought, word and deed which somehow denies Your clear Words, "Given and shed for you for the forgiveness of sins." By the waters of my Baptism, the pronouncement of Holy Absolution, and the preaching of Your life, death, and resurrection for me, prepare me to receive Your Holy Sacrament worthily and for its benefits of forgiveness, life, and salvation.

It is troubling, Lord, that there are those, even friends and family, who cannot receive the Sacrament with me because they do not discern Your Body and Blood, because they belong to a church where Your Word is not taught purely, or because they have not yet been baptized and brought into Your kingdom. I pray, Lord, that You would send Your Holy Spirit so that by Your Word they might learn to believe what is right and true about the gift You give to me in this Supper. Teach me to love them in such a way that I do not ignore what they believe as if it is not important, but that I give a glad and confident witness to the truth that You have promised to give me and that sets me free. Lead those who deny Your words to repentance and faith and bring them also into the joyful fellowship of Your Church so that together with them I may receive Your Body and Blood and share in the fellowship of these holy gifts. Here, Lord, I ask this especially for *(names)*. Bless my pastors too that they may faithfully administer Your Body and Blood to those who are prepared to receive it and faithfully teach Your Word to those who are not yet prepared so that they may be gathered around Your altar also.

Lord, bless the catechumens of my church who are being instructed in the faith, *(especially names)*. Stir up their hearts to hunger and thirst for Your Body and Blood. Bless Your pastors who instruct them that they may do so faithfully. May it never be, Lord, that they think their preparation for the Sacrament is in their learning of their lessons. Rather, let the learning of Your Word teach them that they are truly worthy and well prepared by teaching them faith in Your Words. Let them learn, and let me remember, that my worthiness is not in making myself worthy, but that in my unworthiness You have invited me because You Yourself have become my righteousness. Give to the catechumens and to me a holy and reverent attitude toward Your worship and especially eating and drinking Your Body and Blood. Let me not receive it in a silly or frivolous way, as if it is not important! On the other hand, protect me from a false piety in which I act gloomily as if Your Body and Blood are no occasion for joy and gladness!

Finally, Lord, bless those who are sick or troubled in any way, especially those who cannot be with Your congregation to receive Your Supper. Hear my prayer for (*names*). Grant that they be also prepared for Your Sacrament by repenting of their sins and holding fast to Your Words that Your Body and Blood are given and shed for them for the forgiveness of sins. Let Your Words and Body and Blood be their strength and comfort against all adversity and difficulty so that, by Your presence in this Supper, they would be rescued from all harm and danger, from all despair and unbelief, and be preserved in the holy faith of Your Church until You come again. As I receive Your Body and Blood, I am proclaiming Your death until You come again. Therefore, by Your Supper, strengthen me in the faith and keep me and Your whole Church until that Last Day when You raise me up and give me eternal life. I ask all of this, Lord Jesus Christ, in Your most holy Name, who with the Father and the Holy Spirit are one God, now and forever. Amen.